Dragon Dictate 2.5

MARIA LANGER

Peachpit Press

Visual QuickStart Guide
Dragon Dictate 2.5
Maria Langer

Peachpit Press
1249 Eighth Street
Berkeley, CA 94710
510/524-2178
510/524-2221 (fax)

Find us on the Web at www.peachpit.com.
To report errors, please send a note to errata@peachpit.com.
Peachpit Press is a division of Pearson Education.

Copyright © 2012 by Maria Langer

Editor: Clifford Colby
Production Coordinator: David Van Ness
Copyeditor: Clifford Colby
Technical Editors: Clifford Colby and Maria Langer
Compositors: Maria Langer and David Van Ness
Indexer: Emily Glossbrenner
Cover Design: RHDG / Riezebos Holzbaur Design Group, Peachpit Press
Interior Design: Peachpit Press
Logo Design: MINE™ www.minesf.com

Notice of Rights

Notice of Liability

The information in this book is distributed on an "As Is" basis, without warranty. While every precaution has been taken in the preparation of the book, neither the author nor Peachpit shall have any liability to any person or entity with respect to any loss or damage caused or alleged to be caused directly or indirectly by the instructions contained in this book or by the computer software and hardware products described in it.

Trademarks

Many of the designations used by manufacturers and sellers to distinguish their products are claimed as trademarks. Where those designations appear in this book, and Peachpit was aware of a trademark claim, the designations appear as requested by the owner of the trademark. All other product names and services identified throughout this book are used in editorial fashion only and for the benefit of such companies with no intention of infringement of the trademark. No such use, or the use of any trade name, is intended to convey endorsement or other affiliation with this book.

ISBN-13: 978-0-321-79385-0
ISBN-10:   0-321-79385-4

9 8 7 6 5 4 3 2 1

Printed and bound in the United States of America

Dedication

To David Van Ness
with many thanks for always making
my books look picture-perfect!

Special Thanks:

To Cliff Colby, for giving me the chance to work on a new project—and for making it such a great one! Not only did he give me something to keep me busy and out of trouble, but he gave me an excuse not to rush home to Arizona's summer heat.

To David Van Ness, for his sharp eye and layout skills. As usual, David helped me find and rescue the widows and orphans, close up unnecessary space, and make sure my figure bubbles were the right color. This book wouldn't be nearly as neat and easy to read without David's help.

To Emily Glossbrenner, for squeezing the indexing of this book into her busy schedule—and for getting it done so quickly!

To the folks at Nuance Communications, Inc., for producing a fantastic dictation program that's sure to make any writer's life a lot easier. A special thanks to David Popovitch at Nuance, for answering a few questions as I was working on the book.

And to Mike, for the usual reasons.

Table of Contents

Table of Tables

Introduction

Dragon Dictate by Nuance Communications, Inc. is a Mac OS application that enables you to use your voice to interact with your computer. Specifically, you can use Dragon Dictate to do the following things:

- Dictate text to be automatically typed into a document.
- Use verbal commands to edit text.
- Speak application commands to control computer operations.
- Use verbal commands to manipulate the pointer to perform commands.

Dragon Dictate works by interpreting the words you speak as either dictation or commands, depending, in part, on the operation mode it is in. It has a huge database of vocabulary words that it accesses quickly to respond to what you say. And if you need to enter text or issue commands that are not included in its database, you can customize Dragon Dictate to add them.

Using This Book

This Visual QuickStart Guide will help you learn Dragon Dictate by providing step-by-step instructions, plenty of illustrations, tables full of useful information, and a generous helping of tips. On these pages, you'll find everything you need to know to get up and running quickly with Dragon Dictate—and a lot more!

This book was designed for page flipping. Use the table of contents or index to find the topics you need help for, learn what you need to know, and get on with your work. If you're brand new to Dragon Dictate, however, I recommend that you begin by reading at least the first two chapters of this book. In them, you'll learn how to set up Dragon Dictate to understand your voice and work with various interface elements so you can access its features.

Are you ready to learn Dragon Dictate? Well, then what are you waiting for? Turn the page and let's get started!

1

Getting Started

When you first install Dragon Dictate, it doesn't know anything about your voice or how your voice sounds with your microphone setup. All it has is its own internal database of vocabulary words and commands. If you just started talking, it would not understand what you are saying.

To use Dictate, you need to train it to understand what your voice sounds like when speaking specific words. This is part of the process of creating a profile.

In this chapter, I begin by telling about two Mac OS options that you'll need to configure before using Dictate. Then I explain what a profile is and how you can create one. Finally, I walk you through the process of training Dictate to recognize your voice.

Keep in mind that this chapter assumes that you have installed and registered Dictate for use on your computer. If you have not yet done this, follow the instructions that came with Dictate to do so before working with the instructions in this chapter.

In This Chapter

Before You Begin

Before you can configure and use Dragon Dictate, you should do two things:

- **Enable access for assistive devices.** Dictate uses Mac OS X Universal Access features to listen to and respond to your voice. These features must be enabled for Dictate to work.

- **Connect a USB microphone and set it as the sound input device for your computer.** Although you may be able to set a microphone on the fly when you create a profile, its better to do it in advance to make sure your computer can access it and will do so by default.

In this section, I explain how to do both of these things.

TIP These instructions assume you have Mac OS X Lion installed on your computer. If you have a different version of Mac OS, these instructions and illustrations may work and look a bit differently.

TIP Dictate requires a USB microphone or other compatible device to work. You can learn more about microphone compatibility at http://nuance.custhelp.com/app/answers/detail/a_id/6078.

TIP Although you can use Dictate with your computer's internal microphone, it is not recommended. The sound input quality and ambient noise is likely to result in interpretation errors while using Dictate.

TIP Dictate can also work with an iPhone or iPad running the Dragon Remote Microphone app. You can learn more about using this app in Appendix B, "Setting Up Dragon Remote Microphone" on page 145.

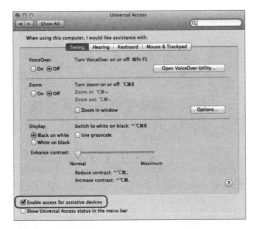

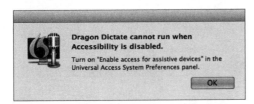

A To use Dictate, you must enable Mac OS for access with assistive devices.

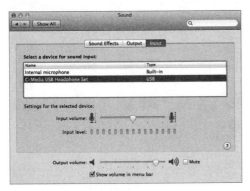

B A warning dialog like this appears if you open Dictate when necessary accessibility features are disabled.

C Select your USB or other compatible microphone in the input options of the Sound preferences pane.

To enable access for assistive devices:

1. Choose Apple > System Preferences to open the System Preferences window.

2. If necessary, click the Show All button in the toolbar to display all preference pane icons.

3. Click the Universal Access icon to display its options **A**.

4. At the bottom of the window, select the check box labeled Enable access for assistive devices **A**.

5. Click the close button to dismiss the preferences window.

TIP If this accessibility option is not enabled, you'll see a warning dialog **B** when you open Dictate. Clicking OK opens Universal Access **A** so you can enable this option.

To connect and set the sound input device:

1. Connect a USB microphone or other compatible microphone to your Mac.

2. Choose Apple > System Preferences to open the System Preferences window.

3. If necessary, click the Show All button in the toolbar to display all preference pane icons.

4. Click the Sound icon.

5. In the Sound preferences pane, click the Input button to display input options **C**.

6. Select the microphone you connected in step 1.

7. Click the close button to dismiss the preferences window.

Creating a Profile

Dragon Dictate uses profiles to distinguish one user/microphone setup from another. This makes it possible for multiple people to use Dictate on the same computer. It also makes it possible for a single user to use Dictate with more than one microphone.

Because it isn't possible to use Dictate without a profile setup, the software will prompt you to set one up right after you install it **A**. After indicating where you want to save the profile and what you want to name it, you provide information about your microphone and go through the process of voice training. Dictate saves the profile as a file on your computer.

You can create multiple profiles for Dictate. Then, when you start the application, you can choose the one that should be used for that session, depending on the user or microphone in use. If you have multiple profiles and no longer need one of them, you can delete it.

TIP You can have more than one microphone set up for a profile. Learn more in the section titled "Managing Profiles & Audio Sources" on page 11.

To create a profile right after installing Dictate:

1. After installing Dictate, it should display the Profiles window with a dialog that prompts you to create a profile **A**. Click Continue.

   A standard Save As dialog appears **B**.

2. Enter a name and choose a location for your profile file.

   The profile appears in the Profiles window **C**.

A When you first install Dictate, it prompts you to create a profile.

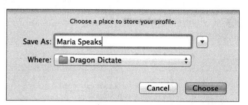

B Use a standard Save As dialog to save the profile file.

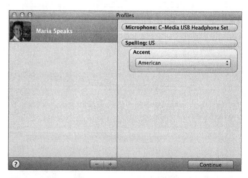

C The new profile and its settings appear in the Profiles window.

D You can choose a microphone from the Microphone pop-up menu.

E Click the button for the spelling you want to use.

F Choose an accent closest to yours. (I never realized that American teens had their own accent.)

3. With the profile selected in the left side of the window, set options in the right side:

   ‣ **Microphone** is the USB or other compatible microphone connected to your computer for use with Dictate. If you have multiple microphones connected, you can use the pop-up menu **D** to select a different one.

   ‣ **Spelling** is the preferred spelling for your language. If English, you can choose US or UK by clicking the appropriate button **E**.

   ‣ **Accent** is your accent. Use the pop-up menu **F** to choose the accent closest to yours.

4. Click Continue.

5. Follow the steps in the section titled "To adjust your microphone" on page 6.

TIP If you have multiple microphones that you plan to use with Dictate, you might want to name your profile based on the microphone it's created for.

To add a profile:

1. If the Profiles window **C** is not already displayed, choose Tools > Profiles to display it.

2. Click the + button at the bottom of the list on the left side of the window.

   A standard Save As dialog appears **B**.

3. Follow steps 2 through 5 in the section titled "To create a profile right after installing Dictate" on page 4 to create the profile.

Adjusting the Microphone

Part of the setup process is to make sure your microphone is properly adjusted so that Dragon Dictate can hear you clearly.

Dictate makes this easy to do by displaying a series of dialogs with instructions. It begins by providing some tips for connecting and positioning your microphone for best results. Then it prompts you to read text while it makes gain adjustments. When it's done, it gives you a chance to review the sound of your voice before accepting the settings and continuing.

TIP Although you can manually adjust the gain settings for your microphone, this is not recommended. It's best to let Dictate listen and make the adjustment automatically for you.

To adjust your microphone:

1. If necessary, follow the steps in the section titled "To create a profile right after installing Dictate" on page 4 or "To add a profile" on page 5 to begin creating a profile.

2. In the Profiles window Ⓐ, click Continue.

3. A dialog that provides instructions for connecting and positioning your microphone appears Ⓑ. Read (to yourself) the advice you'll find there and adjust your microphone accordingly.

4. Click OK.

   Dictate creates a profile file. It displays a status window as it works Ⓒ.

Ⓐ The Profiles window with one profile created.

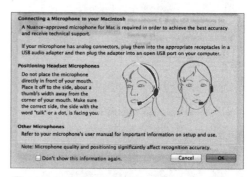

Ⓑ Dragon Dictate offers some advice for using your microphone.

Ⓒ Wait while Dragon Dictate sets up the profile file.

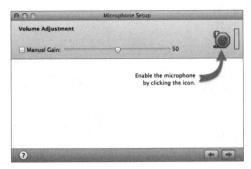

D Click the red icon in the Microphone Setup window.

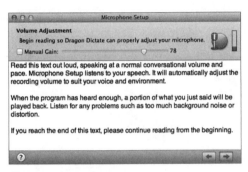

E The window fills with text for you to read.

F When Dictate has heard enough, it tells you it's finished and plays back part of what you read.

5. In the Microphone Setup dialog that appears **D**, click the red icon to enable the microphone.

   The icon turns green and the window fills with text **E**.

6. Begin reading (aloud) the text in the window.

   As you speak, the level indicator shows the recording level and the gain slider automatically adjusts.

   When Dictate has heard enough, the screen changes to indicate that it is finished **F** and it begins playing back the last bit of what you read.

7. Listen to the recording and then:

   ▸ If the recording sounds OK to you, click Stop.

   ▸ If the recording sounds weak or distorted or has a lot of background noise, click the left arrow button at the bottom of the window. Then repeat steps 4 through 7 until you are happy with the sound.

8. Click the Voice Training button at the bottom of the Microphone Setup window **F**.

   The Voice Training window with instructions appears.

9. Continue following the steps in the section titled "To train Dictate to understand your voice" on page 8.

Doing Voice Training

You use voice training to teach Dragon Dictate about how you talk. The voice training process requires you to read specific text into your microphone while Dictate listens. This process normally takes only a few minutes to complete.

Dictate indicates whether it understands you by color-coding the text green or red. If it doesn't understand you, you will have to read the red colored passage again. This process not only teaches Dictate how you speak but also gives you a good idea of how you will dictate text that you want transcribed.

Voice training is part of the profile creation process. You cannot skip it. Fortunately, you only need to do it once for a profile. If, however, you feel that Dictate cannot understand you as well as it should, you can do additional training at any time to improve its recognition capabilities.

To train Dictate to understand your voice:

1. If necessary, follow the steps earlier in this chapter to begin creating a profile and adjust your microphone.

2. Read (to yourself) the instructions in the Voice Training window **A** that appears and click the right arrow button.

3. In the screen that appears **B**, click the red icon to activate your microphone.

   The first screen of text appears **C**.

4. Read the text (aloud). As you read, a few things happen:

   ▸ A progress indicator on the top-left of the window shows your progress.

   ▸ The gain indicator on the top-right of the window shows the sound level.

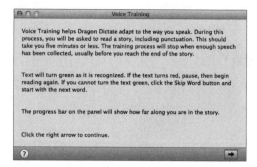

A The first screen of the Voice Training window provides basic instructions.

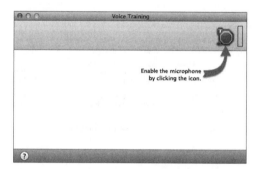

B Click the red icon to activate the microphone.

C The first screen of text appears.

D When Dictate recognizes what you said, the text turns green.

E New text appears when you have successfully read the previous text.

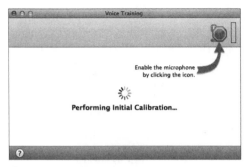

F Dictate tells you when it is performing its initial calibration.

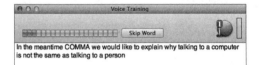

G Then it gives you more text to read aloud.

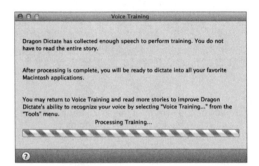

H Dictate processes the training.

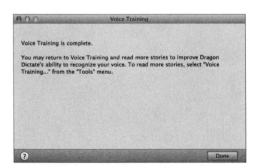

I When training is complete, click Done to dismiss the window.

▸ Text that is understood by Dictate turns green **D**.

▸ Text that is not understood by Dictate turns red. You will have to read this text again.

▸ When all the text on the screen turns green, new text appears **E**.

TIP If you get stuck on a word you can't pronounce, you can click the **Skip Word** button to skip it.

5. Continue reading (aloud) until a screen appears telling you that Dictate is performing its initial calibration **F**.

6. When the "Performing Initial Calibration" message disappears, click the red icon to start the microphone again.

   New text appears in the window **G**.

7. Read the text (aloud) as discussed in step 4. Quite a few screens will appear.

8. When Dictate has heard enough, it tells you **H**. Stop reading and wait for processing to finish.

9. When voice training is complete, a message appears in the window **I**. Click Done.

   The Voice Training window disappears and a status window for the current profile appears **J**. You're now ready to use Dictate with that profile.

J When the status window for a profile appears, Dictate is ready to use.

To do additional voice training:

1. With Dictate open and a profile active, choose Tools > Voice Training.

   The Voice Training window appears .

2. Read (to yourself) the text in the window and click the right arrow button.

   A list of stories appears **K**.

TIP A green icon appears beside each story you have already completed for training.

3. Select the story you want to use for training and click the right arrow button.

4. In the screen that appears **B**, click the red icon to activate your microphone.

   The first screen of text appears **L**.

5. Read the text (aloud). As you read, a few things happen:

   ▸ A progress indicator on the top-left of the window shows your progress.

   ▸ The gain indicator on the top-right of the window shows the sound level.

   ▸ Text that is understood by Dictate turns green **L**.

   ▸ Text that is not understood by Dictate turns red. You will have to read this text again.

   ▸ When all the text on the screen turns green, new text appears **M**.

TIP If you get stuck on a word you can't pronounce, you can click the Skip Word button to skip it.

6. When Dictate has heard enough, it tells you **H**. Stop reading and wait for processing to finish.

7. When voice training is complete, a message appears in the window **I**. Click Done.

K You can choose from among several stories.

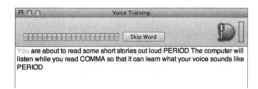

L The first screen of text in Children's Stories.

M The second screen of text in Children's Stories.

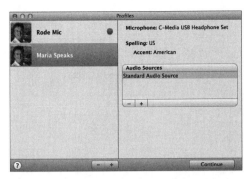

A In this example, there are two profiles, each for the same person but with a different microphone.

B Click OK in this dialog box to delete the selected profile.

Managing Profiles & Audio Sources

Once you have at least one profile set up, you can use the Profiles window to manage your profiles and audio sources.

As discussed in the section titled "To add a profile" on page 5, you can use this window to add a new profile for yourself or another user. As you might imagine, you can also delete a profile from this window.

You can use the Profiles window to add or remove audio sources for individual profiles. And finally, if you have multiple profiles or audio sources, you use this window to choose the one(s) you want to use.

TIP *Audio source* is another term for **microphone.**

To delete a profile:

1. If the Profiles window **A** is not already displayed, choose Tools > Profiles to display it.

2. Select the profile you want to delete **A**.

3. Click the – button at the bottom of the profiles list.

4. In the confirmation dialog that appears **B**, click OK.

   The selected profile is removed.

TIP Why would you remove a profile? One reason is if you know you'll never use that collection of settings—user, microphone, spelling, and accent—ever again.

To add an audio source to a profile:

1. Connect the microphone you want to add to your computer.

2. If the Profiles window  is not already displayed, choose Tools > Profiles to display it.

3. If necessary, select the profile you want to add an audio source to **(A)**.

4. Click the + button at the bottom of the Audio Sources list.

5. In the dialog that appears **(C)**, provide the following information:

   ▸ **Name** is the name of the audio source. You should probably name it after the microphone.

   ▸ **Microphone** is the microphone you want to add. Choose an option from the pop-up menu.

6. Click Continue.

7. A dialog that provides instructions for connecting and positioning your microphone may appear. Read (to yourself) the advice you'll find there and adjust your microphone accordingly.

8. Click OK.

9. Follow steps 5 through 9 in the section titled "To adjust your microphone" on page 6.

10. Continue following the steps in the section titled "To train Dictate to understand your voice" on page 8.

11. When you are finished configuring the new audio device, it is activated for use.

(C) Provide basic information about an audio source in this dialog.

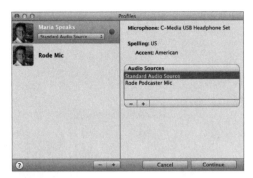

D Select the profile and audio source in the Profiles window.

E Click OK to confirm that you want to delete the audio source.

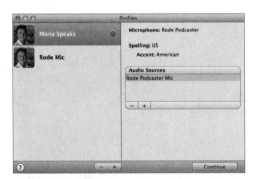

F When you remove a second audio source from a profile, the pop-up menu of sources disappears.

G Use the pop-up menu to choose an audio source for a profile that has multiple audio sources.

To delete an audio source:

1. If the Profiles window **D** is not already displayed, choose Tools > Profiles to display it.

2. If necessary, select the profile with the audio source you want to delete **D**.

3. In the Audio Sources list on the right side of the window, select the source you want to delete.

4. Click the – button at the bottom of the Audio Sources list.

5. In the confirmation dialog that appears **E**, click OK.

6. The audio source is removed from the list and the pop-up menu beneath the profile name disappears **F**.

To select a profile & audio source:

1. Choose Tools > Profiles to display the Profiles window **D**.

2. If necessary, select the profile you want to use **D**.

3. If necessary, use one of the following techniques to select the audio source you want to use:

   ▸ Choose the audio source name from the pop-up menu beneath the profile name **G**.

   ▸ Select the name of the source in the Audio Sources list on the right side of the window **D**.

4. Click Continue to begin using the profile and microphone you selected.

TIP You cannot use a profile or audio source until you complete all of the configuration, including voice training.

Using the Dragon Dictate Interface

Dragon Dictate's interface is simple and designed to be unobtrusive, especially when using it with other applications.

While the Dictate application is active, it offers the usual collection of menus and windows for setting options and working with certain application features. When another application is active, however, its interface is limited to a few translucent windows and a menu bar icon — all of which can be hidden if you prefer not to see them.

This chapter introduces the Dictate interface and explains how you can use each of its elements to work with the application. It also tells you how to perform a few basic tasks that you'll use every time you work with Dictate.

In This Chapter

Interface Elements

Dragon Dictate's interface can be broken down into a number of elements, including menus, windows, and keyboard shortcuts. Let's take a closer look at them.

Menus

Like most Mac OS applications, Dictate makes extensive use of menus to access commands and open windows:

- **Menu bar menus** appear at the top of the screen. Click a menu to display it **A**; click a command to choose it.

Status icon

A The menu bar includes Dictate's menus, including a status menu icon.

B C The status menu icon indicates whether the microphone is off (left) or on (right).

TIP You can find all of Dictate's menus illustrated in Appendix A.

- A **status menu icon** also appears on the menu bar at the top of the screen **A**. The appearance of this icon indicates whether the microphone is turned off **A B** or on **C**. Click the icon to toggle the microphone on or off.

- A **Dock menu** is available on the Dock when Dictate is open. Point to the Dictate Dock icon and hold down the button to display the menu **D**. This menu includes options for commonly used commands and offers a quick way to switch from one open window to another.

D Dictate's Dock menu offers quick access to commonly used commands.

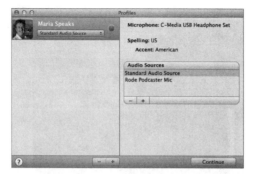

E Use the Profiles window to open, add, or modify a profile or audio source.

F The Status window provides information about Dictate's status and lets you change modes.

Full screen button

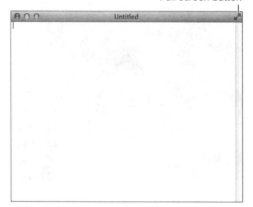

G The Note Pad window is a simple text document window that you can use to record dictated text.

Windows

Dictate includes a number of windows you use to work with the application and its features:

- **Profiles window E** lists all profiles created for Dictate, along with the audio sources for each. The Profiles window appears automatically when you open Dictate, but you can open it at any time by choosing Tools > Profiles.

TIP Using the Profiles window is covered in detail in Chapter 1.

- **Status window F** floats over all other application windows, giving you constant information about Dictate's status whenever Dictate is open. You can use the Status window to toggle the microphone on or off, change modes, and confirm which application or window Dictate is working with.

TIP Although it's always a good idea to have the Status window showing while you're using Dictate, you can toggle its display by choosing Window > Hide Status Window or Window > Show Status Window.

- **Note Pad window G**, which appears automatically when you open Dictate, is a text window you can use to record dictated text. To open a new Note Pad window choose File > New Note Pad or press Command-N.

TIP Dictate supports Mac OS X Lion's full screen view feature. To activate it, click the Full Screen button in the upper-right corner of any Note Pad window G, choose Window > Enter Full Screen, or press Control-Command-F. You can learn more about Lion's features in my book *Mac OS X Lion: Visual QuickStart Guide*.

continues on next page

- **Available Commands window**  is a floating window that lists commands currently available in Dictate. Commands are organized by application and topic; click a disclosure triangle to display or hide subitems. You can also use a Spotlight search box at the top of the window to search for specific commands. To toggle the display of the Available Commands window, choose Window > Show Available Commands or Window > Hide Available Commands.

- **Recognition window**  is a floating window that enables you to help Dictate understand text you have spoken. In some cases, this window appears automatically, but you can also toggle its display from the Status window or with a hot key.

TIP **Working with the Recognition window is covered in detail in the section titled "Using the Recognition Window" on page 60.**

H The Available Commands window is a quick reference guide to the commands you can use with Dictate.

I You can use the Recognition window to help Dictate understand what you said. In this example, I said "this is a test" and that's what Dictate thinks I probably said. But it also offers other possibilities that could be right.

TABLE 2.1 Default Global Hot Keys

Task	Keystroke
Toggle Microphone	Command-F11
Select Speech Mode	Command-F10
Show Recognition Window	Command-F9
Dismiss MouseGrid	Command-F12

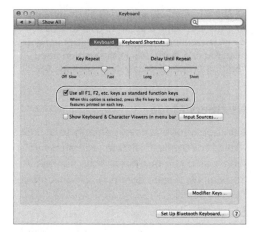

J You must turn on this option in the Keyboard preferences pane to use Dictate's default global hot keys.

Keyboard Shortcuts

Dictate supports two kinds of keyboard shortcuts:

- **Command shortcuts** enable you to choose menu commands with your keyboard. In most cases, command shortcuts appear on menus **A**.

TIP Keyboard shortcuts for Dictate's menu commands are listed in Appendix A.

- **Global hot keys** (Table 2.1) enable you to perform common tasks with simple keystrokes.

TIP Global hot keys can be modified in Dictate preferences, as discussed in the section titled "Shortcuts Preferences" on page 138.

TIP To use the default global hot keys or any hot keys that incorporate the function keys on a keyboard, turn on the option labeled "Use all F1, F2, etc. keys as standard function keys" in the Mac OS X Keyboard preferences pane **J**.

Modes

Dragon Dictate offers five different modes of operation. The mode Dictate is in determines what you can say and what happens when you say it.

TIP You can set options in Dictate preferences to specify which mode Dictate starts in. You can learn more about setting preferences in the section titled "General Preferences" on page 133.

Dictation Mode

Dictation mode is used primarily for dictating text. Dictated text is recorded at the insertion point in the active document window or field. If Dictate recognizes a valid command, however, it performs that command's task instead of typing the command's words.

Command Mode

Command mode is used to issue commands to your computer. Although you can also issue commands in Dictation, Spelling, or Numbers mode, when you're in Command mode, Dictate doesn't have to determine whether you're dictating or spelling something. Instead, it listens for commands and if it recognizes one, it performs the command's task. If you say something in Command mode that Dictate does not recognize, nothing happens.

Spelling Mode

Spelling mode is used primarily to spell out text you want Dictate to type. You might use this mode to spell out unusual words or acronyms. In this mode, Dictate recognizes a limited set of letters and punctuation; if it hears them, it types them. But if it recognizes a valid command, it performs that command's task instead.

TIP If you find yourself using Spelling mode to enter the same text string over and over, consider adding that text to Dictate's vocabulary. You can learn how in the section titled "Editing Dictate's Vocabulary" on page 68.

Numbers Mode

Numbers mode is used primarily to dictate Arabic numerals. If Dictate recognizes your words as a number, it types the number. You can also issue commands in this mode.

Sleep Mode

Sleep mode is used to pause Dictate without turning off the microphone. In Sleep mode, Dictate recognizes only two commands, either of which will return you to the previously used mode:

- *Wake Up*
- *Turn [the] Microphone On*

TIP The benefit of Sleep mode over turning the microphone off is that you can use voice commands to resume work with Dictate. If you turn off the microphone, as discussed in the section titled "To turn the microphone off" on page 22, you must use your hands (instead of your voice) to resume work.

 B The Status menu icon is red when the microphone is off.

A The Microphone button in the Status window is red when the microphone is off.

C The Speech menu looks like this when the microphone is off.

D The Dragon Dictate Dock menu looks like this when the microphone is off.

E The Microphone button in the Status window is green when the microphone is on.

 F The Status menu icon is green when the microphone is on.

Performing Common Tasks

As you work with Dragon Dictate, you'll find yourself performing the same basic tasks over and over: turning the microphone on and off, switching modes, checking Dictate status.

This part of the chapter reviews all of these tasks. Take a moment to practice them before moving on to the next chapter and working with Dictate.

To turn the microphone on:

Use one of the following techniques:

- Click the red Microphone button in the Status window **A**.

- Click Dragon Dictate's red Status menu icon **B**

- With Dragon Dictate active, choose Speech > Microphone On **C**, or press Command-F11.

- Choose Microphone On from the Dragon Dictate Dock menu **D**.

The icon in the Status window **E** and on Dictate's Status menu turns to a green go button **F**.

To turn the microphone off:

Use one of the following techniques:

- Say *Microphone Off*.
- Click the green Microphone button in the Status window **E**.
- Click Dragon Dictate's green Status menu icon **F**.
- Choose Speech > Microphone Off **G**, or press Command-F11.
- Choose Microphone Off from the Dragon Dictate Dock menu **H**.

The icon in the Status window **A** and on Dictate's Status menu turns to a red stop button **B**.

To switch to a different mode:

Use one of the following techniques:

- Say one of the following commands:
  - ▸ *Dictation Mode*
  - ▸ *Command Mode*
  - ▸ *Spelling Mode*
  - ▸ *Numbers Mode*
  - ▸ *Sleep Mode*
- Choose the mode you want from the Status window's Mode menu **I**.
- Choose the mode you want from the Speech menu **C G**.
- Choose the mode you want from the Dragon Dictate Dock menu **D H**.

The Mode menu icon in the Status menu changes accordingly **E J K L M**.

TIP If Dictate is in Sleep mode, you must wake it before switching to a different mode. Learn how in the section titled "To wake from Sleep mode" on page 23.

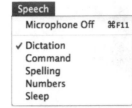

G The Speech menu looks like this when the microphone is on.

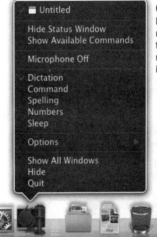

H The Dragon Dictate Dock menu looks like this when the microphone is on.

I The Mode menu in the Status window offers one way to switch from one mode to another.

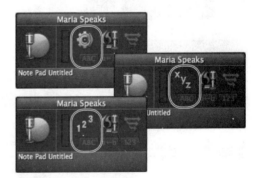

J K L The Mode menu's icon indicates the mode: Command (top), Spelling (middle), and Numbers (bottom). **E** shows Dictation mode.

M The Status window looks like this in Sleep mode.

N When Dictate is asleep, there's only one option on the Mode menu in the Status window.

 O The Status menu icon looks like this when Dictate is asleep.

P When Dictate is asleep, the Speech menu only offers two commands.

Q The Dragon Dictate Dock menu looks like this when Dictate is asleep.

To wake from Sleep mode:

Use one of the following techniques:

- Say one of the following:
  - ▸ *Wake Up*
  - ▸ *Turn [the] Microphone On*
- Click the purple Microphone button in the Status window **M**.
- Choose Wake Up from the Status window's Mode menu **N**.
- Click Dragon Dictate's purple Status menu icon **O**.
- Choose Speech > Microphone On or Speech > Wake Up **P**, or press Command-F11.
- Choose Microphone On or Wake Up from the Dragon Dictate Dock menu **Q**.

Dictate wakes from Sleep mode and turns the microphone on. The status icons change accordingly **E G**.

To determine Dictate's status:

Examine the microphone button in the Status window **A D J** or the Status menu icon **B F K** to see what color and icon appears:

- A red stop sign **A B** means the microphone is off.
- A green go button **E F** means the microphone is on.
- A purple moon **M O** means Dictate is in Sleep mode.

3

Dictating Text

Dragon Dictate's main strength is the ability to interpret the words it hears and transcribe the resulting text. This makes it an excellent tool for taking dictation. In fact, there's a good chance that the only Dictate features you'll use regularly are its dictation features.

Dictate offers three modes for taking dictation: Dictation, Spelling, and Numbers modes. In most cases, you'll use Dictation mode, but you may find the Spelling and Numbers modes handy for dictating unusual words or long lists of numbers.

This chapter explains how to use Dictate to transcribe the text you speak. Along the way, it explains how to include line breaks and punctuation and set capitalization and spacing. It also tells you how you can spell out words and enter numbers.

To make the most of this chapter, you'll need to know the information in Chapter 2. If you skipped over that chapter, go back and read it now.

This chapter will concentrate on *dictating* text; *editing* text using spoken commands is covered in Chapter 4.

In This Chapter

Using the Note Pad

Although you can use Dragon Dictate to transcribe what you say into documents for virtually any application—for example, Microsoft Word, Apple Pages, TextEdit, or Mail—Dictate also includes its own internal text editing feature: Note Pad. In fact, when you open Dictate, it automatically opens an empty Note Pad window for your use 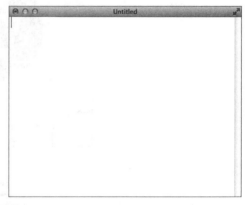.

To have Dictate type into the Note Pad window, all you need to do is make sure the window is active when you begin dictation. The text you speak will be inserted in the document at the insertion point. This works not only for dictation, as discussed in this chapter, but for editing text, as discussed in Chapter 4.

When you're finished working on a Note Pad document, you'll probably want to save it. This makes it possible to open and edit the file at a later date or to use it with another application.

As you might expect, you create, save, close, and open a Note Pad file as you would any other document file: by using commands under the File menu **B**.

TIP The instructions in this chapter assume you will dictate into a Dragon Dictate Note Pad window **A**. You can, however, use the same instructions with any other application.

TIP You can use Dictate's Command mode to save, close, open, and perform other tasks with Note Pad files using verbal commands. Learn more about using Command mode to work with the Dictate application in Chapter 6.

To create a Note Pad file:

Choose File > New Note Pad **B**, or press Command-N.

An empty, untitled Note Pad window appears **A**.

A You can dictate text into any document window, including a Dragon Dictate Note Pad window like this one.

B Dictate's File menu includes commands for working with Note Pad files.

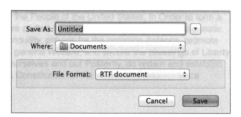

C Use the Save As dialog to save a Note Pad file for later use.

D You can also open an RTF or plain text file within Dictate to modify it in a Note Pad window.

To save a Note Pad file for the first time:

1. With the Note Pad window active, choose File > Save or File > Save As B, or press Command-S.

2. In the Save As dialog that appears C, enter a name, select a disk location, and choose a file format for the file.

3. Click Save.

TIP Remember, in step 2 you can click the disclosure triangle to the right of the Save As field to expand the dialog and offer more options for choosing a disk location in which to save the file. This is a standard Mac OS feature.

TIP Dictate's Note Pad can save files as RTF (Rich Text Format) or Plain Text documents. If your document includes formatting, be sure to save it as an RTF file.

To save changes to a Note Pad file:

With the Note Pad window active, choose File > Save B, or press Command-S.

Your changes are saved.

To open an existing text file:

1. With Dictate active, choose File > Open B, or press Command-O.

2. In the Open dialog that appears D, locate and select the file you want to open.

3. Click Open.

TIP You can open any plain text or RTF file within Dictate—not just files created and saved with Dictate.

Dictating Text

Dictating text is easy. All you do is say what you want transcribed. Dragon Dictate listens to what you say and types it for you.

There are a few things to keep in mind when dictating text:

- Make sure you're in the right mode for the type of dictation you want to do. In most cases, this will be Dictation mode, but it could also be Spelling or Numbers mode.

TIP You can learn more about Dictate's modes in the section titled "Modes" on page 20.

- Speak smoothly and continuously to help Dictate recognize spoken text as dictation.

- In Dictation mode, Dictate will automatically insert spaces between words and after punctuation as appropriate. You can use commands to override Dictate's automatic spacing.

- To issue a command while dictating, pause, say a valid command, and wait for Dictate to react. It should interpret what you say as a command rather than dictation.

- Use the correct commands for punctuation, capitalization, and non-word characters such as symbols.

- If Dictate types the wrong word or phrase for something you just said, you can say *Delete That* to remove it. Think of this as an undo command for dictation.

This section explains how to dictate text and provides lists of commands you'll find useful when doing so.

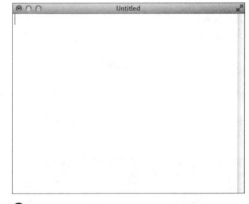

A You can dictate text into any document window, including a Dragon Dictate Note Pad window like this one.

B This Status window indicates the microphone is on and Dictate is in Dictation mode.

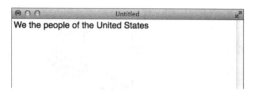

We the people of the United States

G Dictate types the text you speak.

Capitalization Indicator

D The capitalization indicator will appear in brown or green, depending on the capitalization command used.

TABLE 3.1 Dictation Capitalization Commands

To capitalize text like this:	Say this:
Capitalize next word	*Cap*
Capitalize all subsequent text	*Caps On*
Stop capitalizing subsequent text	*Caps Off*
Type next word in uppercase letters	*All Caps*
Type all subsequent text in uppercase letters	*All Caps On*
Stop typing all subsequent text in uppercase letters	*All Caps Off*
Type next word in lowercase letters	*No Caps*
Type all subsequent text in lowercase letters	*No Caps On*
Stop typing all subsequent text in lowercase letters	*No Caps Off*

To dictate text:

1. Position the insertion point in the document where you want text to appear **A**.

2. If necessary, turn on the microphone.

   A green Go button appears in the Status window **B**.

3. If necessary, switch to Dictation mode.

4. Say the text you want transcribed.

   Each time you pause, Dictate types the text you just said **G**.

To set capitalization while dictating:

1. Say the command for the capitalization you want (Table 3.1).

   The capitalization indicator in the Status window **D** changes color accordingly:

   ▸ If you said a command that affects just the next word, the indicator turns brown.

   ▸ If you said a command that affects all subsequent text, the indicator turns green.

2. Say the word(s) you want the capitalization command applied to.

3. If necessary, say the command to end the capitalization.

   When capitalization settings are back to normal, the capitalization indicator turns gray again **B**.

TIP Dictate's built-in dictionary can automatically capitalize proper nouns, acronyms, and many other commonly used words.

To exclude spaces while dictating:

1. Say the command for the spacing option you want (Table 3.2).

   If you used one of the No Space commands, the spacing indicator in the Status window **E** changes color accordingly:

   ▸ If you said **No Space**, the indicator turns brown.

   ▸ If you said **No Space On**, the indicator turns green.

2. Say the word(s) you want the capitalization command applied to.

3. If necessary, say **No Space Off** to return spacing to normal for subsequent text.

   When spacing settings are back to normal, the spacing indicator turns gray again **B**.

To type spaces, punctuation, or symbols while dictating:

Pause and then say the command for the space (Table 3.3), punctuation (Table 3.4), or symbol (Table 3.5, Table 3.11, and Table 3.13) you want.

TIP You can also insert punctuation while editing text. Learn how in the section titled "Adding Punctuation to Existing Text" on page 55.

To stop dictating:

Use one of the following techniques:

- Switch to Sleep mode, as discussed in the section titled "To switch to a different mode" on page 22.

- Turn off the microphone, as discussed in the section titled "To turn the microphone off" on page 22.

Spacing indicator

E The spacing indicator will appear in brown or green, depending on the spacing command used.

TABLE 3.2 Commands for Excluding Spaces

To include or exclude spaces like this:	Say this:
Prevent the automatic insertion of a space before the next word	**No Space**
Disable the automatic inclusion of spaces between subsequent words	**No Space On**
Stop disabling the automatic inclusion of spaces between subsequent words	**No Space Off**

TABLE 3.3 Space Commands

To include this kind of space:	Say this:	Mode D	S	N
Space	**Space Bar**	X	X	X
Non-breaking (or "sticky" space)	**No-Break Space** or **Non-Breakable Space**		X	
Tab	**Tab Key**	X		X
New line *	**New Line** or **Next Line**	X		X
New paragraph **	**New Paragraph** or **Next Paragraph**	X		X

* Single return character
** Double return character

TABLE 3.4 Punctuation Commands

To type this:	Say this:	D	S	N
.	Period or Full Stop or Dot	X	X	X
.	Period Paragraph	X		X
!	Exclamation Mark or Exclamation Point	X		X
¡	Inverted Exclamation Point	X	X	
?	Question Mark	X	X	X
¿	Inverted Question Mark	X	X	
,	Comma	X	X	X
;	Semicolon	X	X	X
:	Colon	X	X	X
·	Center Dot	X	X	
-	Hyphen	X	X	X
-	Soft Hyphen		X	
--	Dash	X	X	
--	En Dash	X		
–	En Dash		X	
---	Em Dash	X		
—	Em Dash		X	
'	Apostrophe	X	X	
's	Apostrophe S	X	X	
'	Open Single Quote or Begin Single Quote		X	
'	Close Single Quote or End Single Quote		X	
'	Single Quote		X	
'	Open Single Quote or Begin Single Quote	X		
'	Close Single Quote or End Single Quote	X		
"	Open Quote or Begin Quote		X	
"	Close Quote or End Quote		X	
"	Quote or Quotation Marks		X	
"	Open Quote or Begin Quote or Open Double Quote or Begin Double Quote	X		

TABLE 3.4 continued

To type this:	Say this:	D	S	N
"	Close Quote or End Quote or Close Double Quote or End Double Quote	X		
«	Open Euro Quote	X	X	
»	Close Euro Quote	X	X	
«	Open Angle Quote or Begin Angle Quote		X	
»	Close Euro Quote or End Angle Quote		X	
(	Open Paren or Open Parenthesis or Left Paren or Left Parenthesis	X	X	X
)	Close Paren or Close Parenthesis or Right Paren or Right Parenthesis	X	X	X
[	Open Bracket or Open Square Bracket or Left Bracket or Left Square Bracket	X	X	
]	Close Bracket or Close Square Bracket or Right Bracket or Right Square Bracket	X	X	
{	Open Brace or Open Curly Brace or Left Brace or Left Curly Brace	X	X	
}	Close Brace or Close Curly Brace or Right Brace or Right Curly Brace	X	X	
<	Open Angle Bracket or Left Angle Bracket	X		
>	Close Angle Bracket or Right Angle Bracket	X		
‹	Open Angle Bracket or Left Angle Bracket		X	
›	Close Angle Bracket or Right Angle Bracket		X	

TABLE 3.5 Symbol Commands

To type this:	Say this:	D	S	N
~	Tilde	X	X	
`	Backquote	X	X	
`	Backtick	X		
@	At Sign	X	X	
@	At		X	
#	Pound Sign or Number Sign	X	X	
#	Pound or Number		X	
^	Caret	X	X	
^	Hat		X	
&	Ampersand or And Sign	X	X	
&	Ampersand Sign		X	
&&	Logical And	X		
*	Asterisk	X	X	X
*	Star		X	
_	Underscore	X	X	X
		Vertical Bar	X	X	
		Bar		X	
¦	Broken Vertical Bar		X	
||	Logical Or	X		
/	Slash or Forward Slash	X	X	X
\	Backslash	X	X	
™	Trademark Sign	X	X	
™	Trademark		X	

TABLE 3.5 *continued*

To type this:	Say this:	D	S	N
§	Section Sign	X	X	
§	Section		X	
¶	Paragraph Sign	X	X	
¶	Paragraph		X	
•	Large Center Dot	X		
°	Degree Sign	X	X	
°	Degree		X	
ª	Feminine Ordinal Sign	X		
ª	Feminine Ordinal		X	
º	Masculine Ordinal		X	
®	Registered Sign	X	X	
®	Registered or Registered Trademark or Registered Trademark Sign		X	
†	Single Dagger Sign	X		
†	Dagger		X	
‡	Double Dagger Sign	X		
‡	Double Dagger		X	
å	Angstrom		X	
©	Copyright Sign	X	X	
©	Copyright		X	
...	Ellipsis or Dot Dot Dot	X		X
...	Ellipsis		X	
μ	Greek Mu	X	X	
μ	Micron		X	

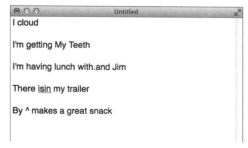

```
●○○                  Untitled
I cloud

I'm getting My Teeth

I'm having lunch with.and Jim

There isin my trailer

By ^ makes a great snack
```

A Here are a few examples of text Dictate misunderstood. (If you try these for yourself, make sure you say *Caps Off* after the second example.) You can use Spelling mode to spell problem words or phrases.

Spelling Text

Dragon Dictate has an extensive vocabulary of words, including many technical terms, proper nouns, acronyms, and abbreviations. Because of this, you should be able to enter most text in Dictation mode without much trouble.

But sometimes you may need to enter text that Dictate either doesn't know or recognizes as a command. For example, when I say *iCloud* (an Apple service), Dictate types *I cloud* **A** because it simply doesn't know the word iCloud. And if I say *I'm getting caps on my teeth*, Dictate types *I'm getting My Teeth* because it recognizes the phrase "caps on" in my sentence as the *Caps On* command.

Try a few for yourself. Say the following to see how you do:

- *I'm having lunch with Dot and Jim*
- *There is no space in my trailer*
- *A carrot makes a great snack*

Clearly, this can cause problems when you dictate certain words or phrases.

Fortunately, Dictate has you covered. It enables you to spell out unusual words or phrases that might be recognized as commands. You do this in Spelling mode.

TIP Although you can usually spell out words within Dictation mode, Spelling mode works more reliably. In Spelling mode, Dictate expects to hear letters and related commands rather than vocabulary words.

TIP If you find yourself spelling the same unusual word over and over, you can add it to Dictate's vocabulary list. You can learn how in the section titled "Editing Dictate's Vocabulary" on page 68.

To spell out a word:

1. If necessary, switch to Spelling mode.

2. Do one of the following:

   ▸ Say the letter you want to type. For example, you can say *A* or *T*.

   ▸ Say the letter's command based on the International Radio Alphabet (Table 3.6). For example, you can say *Alpha* or *Tango*.

   ▸ Say a diacritical letter's command (Table 3.7).

   ▸ Say a ligature or non-latin letter's command (Table 3.8).

3. Repeat this process to spell the entire word.

4. To spell multiple words, be sure to say *Space Bar* between them.

TABLE 3.6 International Radio Alphabet

To type this:	Say this:	To type this:	Say this:
a	*Alpha*	n	*November*
b	*Bravo*	o	*Oscar*
c	*Charlie*	p	*Papa*
d	*Delta*	q	*Quebec*
e	*Echo*	r	*Romeo*
f	*Foxtrot*	s	*Sierra*
g	*Golf*	t	*Tango*
h	*Hotel*	u	*Uniform*
i	*India*	v	*Victor*
j	*Juliet*	w	*Whiskey*
k	*Kilo*	x	*Xray*
l	*Lima*	y	*Yankee*
m	*Mike*	z	*Zulu*

TABLE 3.7 Commands for Diacritical Letters

To type this:	Say this:	To type this:	Say this:
á	*Alpha [Accent] Acute*	ï	*India [Accent] Umlaut*
â	*Alpha [Accent] Circumflex*	ñ	*November [Accent] Tilde*
à	*Alpha [Accent] Grave*	ó	*Oscar [Accent] Acute*
ã	*Alpha [Accent] Tilde*	ô	*Oscar [Accent] Circumflex*
ä	*Alpha [Accent] Umlaut*	ò	*Oscar [Accent] Grave*
å	*Alpha Ring [Above]*	õ	*Oscar [Accent] Tilde*
ç	*Charlie [Accent] Cedilla*	ö	*Oscar [Accent] Umlaut*
é	*Echo [Accent] Acute*	ø	*Oscar Oblique Stroke*
ê	*Echo [Accent] Circumflex*	ú	*Uniform [Accent] Acute*
è	*Echo [Accent] Grave*	û	*Uniform [Accent] Circumflex*
ë	*Echo [Accent] Umlaut*	ù	*Uniform [Accent] Grave*
í	*India [Accent] Acute*	ü	*Uniform [Accent] Umlaut*
î	*India [Accent] Circumflex*	ý	*Yankee [Accent] Acute*
ì	*India [Accent] Grave*	ÿ	*Yankee [Accent] Umlaut*

TABLE 3.8 Commands for Ligatures &
Non-Latin Characters

To type this:	Say this:
æ	*A E Ligature*
œ	*O E Ligature*
ß	*Eszet* or *German Sharp S*
š	*S With Caron* or *S Wedge*
ð	*Icelandic Eth*
þ	*Icelandic Thorn*

- To dictate commands for diacritical letters in Dictation mode, be sure to say *Accent* as indicated (Table 3.7). This word is not required in Spelling mode.

- Note that not all fonts support a full set of diacritical letters, ligatures, or non-Latin characters. If the font you are using does not support a letter you type by dictation, it may not appear as expected.

- Some characters are simply impossible to type by dictating them. Instead, you can set up a Text Macro command. You can learn how in the section titled "Adding Custom Commands" on page 123.

Tips for spelling success:

Here are some additional tips for successfully spelling out text:

- To immediately remove an incorrect letter, say *Scratch That*. You can then try again to say the correct letter.

- Dictated letters are uppercase by default in Dictation mode and lowercase by default in Spelling mode. If a letter appears at the beginning of a sentence in Spelling mode, however, it may be automatically capitalized.

- Be sure to include any other commands you might need to type the word. For example, to type *iCloud* at the beginning of a sentence or line, you'll need to say: *No Caps India Cap Charlie Lima Oscar Uniform Delta*. Note that you could also type this in Dictation mode by saying: *No Caps India No Space Cap Cloud*.

- Another way to type an uppercase letter in Spelling mode is to use the command *Capital* or *Uppercase*. So, for example, to type an uppercase letter A, you could say: *Capital A*, *Capital Alpha*, *Uppercase A*, or *Uppercase Alpha*.

- To type initials separated by a period and a space, be sure to say *Period Space Bar* between them. So to enter my initials (*M. L.*), you could say: *Capital Mike Period Space Bar Capital Lima Period*.

- To type an acronym, say the letters of the acronym without spaces. So, to type *FAR* (short for *Federal Aviation Regulation*), you could say: *Capital F Capital A Capital R*.

To combine dictation with spelling:

1. Switch to the mode you want to use.

2. Say the words or letters you need to type the word or words.

3. Repeat steps 1 and 2 to dictate and spell the text.

Table 3.9 tells you what to say to type the examples on page 33.

TABLE 3.9 Examples Combining Dictation and Spelling Modes

To type this:	Say this:
I'm getting caps on my teeth.	*Dictation Mode I'm getting Spelling Mode Space Bar Charlie Alpha Papa Sierra Space Bar Dictation Mode on my teeth Period*
I'm having lunch with Dot and Jim.	*Dictation Mode I'm having lunch with Spelling Mode Space Bar Cap Delta Oscar Tango Space Bar Dictation Mode and Jim Period*
There is no space in my trailer.	*Dictation Mode There is Spelling Mode Space Bar November Oscar Space Bar Dictation Mode space in my trailer Period*
	(Note that you could also type this sentence by saying: *There is no* [pause] *space in my trailer Period*)
A carrot is a good snack.	*Dictation Mode A Spelling Mode Charlie Alpha Romeo Romeo Oscar Tango Space Bar Dictation Mode snack Period*
	(To be fair, sometimes you can just say this sentence slowly and clearly in Dictation mode and it will be typed correctly.)

TABLE 3.10 Dictating Numbers in Dictation Mode

To type this:	Say this:
1	*Numeral One* or *One*
12	*One Two* or *Twelve*
437	*Four Three Seven* or *Four hundred and thirty seven*
6,498	*Six Comma No Space Four Nine Eight* or *Six thousand four hundred and ninety eight*
24,616	*Two Four Comma No Space Six One Six* or *Twenty four thousand six hundred and sixteen*
137.34	*One Three Seven Point Three Four* or *One hundred and thirty seven point thirty four*
6.02	*Six Point Zero Two*
43%	*Four Three Percent Sign* or *Forty three percent*
87.98%	*Eight Seven Point Nine Eight Percent Sign* or *Eighty seven Point Ninety eight percent*
6 million	*Six million*
12.4 billion	*Twelve Point four billion*

Dictating Numbers

In addition to typing text with related punctuation and symbols, you can also use Dragon Dictate to type numbers, fractions, and mathematical operators.

Although Dictate includes a Numbers mode for entering numbers, most numbers can be accurately entered in Dictation mode. This part of the chapter explains how to enter them in either mode.

TIP To immediately remove an incorrect digit, say *Scratch Number* or *Scratch That*. You can then try again to say the correct digit.

To dictate numbers in Dictation mode:

In Dictation mode, do one of the following:

- Say each digit of the number you want to enter. If you want to include a comma or decimal point, be sure to say *Comma No Space* or *Point* in the correct place.

- Say the full name of the number in one smooth phrase.

Table 3.10 shows examples of numbers and what you can say to dictate them.

TIP To ensure that Dictate types a single-digit number as an Arabic number instead of a word, say *Numeral* before it (Table 3.10).

To dictate in Numbers mode:

1. Switch to Numbers mode.

2. Say a digit you want to type.

3. Repeat this process to enter the entire number.

TIP To type multiple numbers, be sure to use some sort of punctuation command between them.

To dictate Roman numerals:

In Dictation mode, say **Roman Numeral** followed by the number that you want typed.

For example, saying **Roman Numeral Twelve** produces *XII*.

TIP To get lowercase characters, you can either spell them out or use the Lowercase command to edit a Roman numeral after it has been typed.

To dictate fractions:

In Dictation mode, say the fraction.

Table 3.11 shows some examples.

TIP It may be necessary to say *Numeral* before single digit fraction numerators. Otherwise, Dictate may spell out the number as a word.

TIP If you have difficulty getting Dictate to recognize a fraction, you can say *Slash* or *Over* between the fraction's numerator or denominator.

To dictate mathematical symbols:

In Dictation or Spelling mode, say the command for the symbol you want (Table 3.12).

TABLE 3.11 Dictating Fractions

To type this:	Say This:
1/2	*Numeral One half* or *Numeral One Over Two*
1/4	*Numeral One Quarter* or *Numeral Over Four*
7/8	*Seven Eighths*
13/32	*Thirteen Thirty Seconds*
4 5/16	*Four and Five Sixteenths*
120/72	*One Twenty Over Seventy Two*

TABLE 3.12 Mathematical Symbol Commands

To type this:	Say this:	D	S	N
=	*Equals Sign*	X	X	
=	*Equals*		X	
+	*Plus Sign*	X	X	X
+	*Plus*		X	
−	*Minus Sign*	X	X	X
±	*Plus or Minus Sign*	X	X	
±	*Plus or Minus* or *Plus Minus* or *Plus Minus Sign*		X	
×	*Multiplication Sign*	X		
×	*Multiply* or *Multiply Sign* or *Times* or *Times Sign*		X	
÷	*Division Sign*	X	X	
÷	*Divide* or *Divide Sign*		X	
<	*Less Than Sign*	X	X	
<	*Less Than*		X	
>	*Greater Than Sign*	X	X	
>	*Greater Than*		X	
%	*Percent Sign*	X	X	
%	*Percent*		X	
¬	*Logical Not Sign*	X	X	
¬	*Not* or *Not Sign* or *Logical Not*		X	
²	*Superscript Two*	X	X	
²	*Square* or *Squared*		X	
³	*Superscript Three*	X	X	
³	*Cube* or *Cubed*		X	
½	*One Half Sign*	X	X	
½	*Half* or *Half Sign* or *One Half*		X	
¼	*One Quarter Sign*	X	X	
¼	*Quarter* or *Quarter Sign* or *One Quarter*		X	
¾	*Three Quarters Sign*	X	X	
¾	*Three Quarters*		X	

TABLE 3.13 Currency Symbol Commands

To type this:	Say this:	Mode		
		D	**S**	**N**
$	*Dollar Sign*	X	X	
$	*Dollar*		X	
¢	*Cents Sign*	X	X	
¢	*Cents*		X	
£	*Pound Sterling Sign*	X		
£	*Sterling or Sterling Sign*		X	
€	*Euro Sign*	X	X	
€	*Euro*		X	
¥	*Yen Sign*	X	X	
¥	*Yen*		X	

TABLE 3.14 Dictating Currency Amounts

To type this:	Say This:
$5	*Five Dollars*
$5.00	*Five Point Zero Zero Dollars*
$12.67	*Twelve Dollars and Sixty Seven Cents* or *Dollar Sign Twelve Point Six Seven*
$.16	*Sixteen Cents*
16 ¢	*Sixteen Cents Sign*
€18	*Eighteen Euros*
€18.24	*Eighteen Euros and Twenty Four Cents*
£416	*Four Hundred and Sixteen Pounds Sterling*
£416.22	*Pounds Sterling Sign Four Hundred and Sixteen Point Two Two*
¥93	*Ninety Three Yen*

Dictating Special Text

In addition to entering plain text and numbers, Dictate also enables you to dictate information that combines text and numbers. This includes currency amounts, phone numbers, dates, times, and addresses with Zip or postal codes.

Dictate not only recognizes these kinds of entries, but can also automatically format them so you don't need to include formatting as part of your dictation.

TIP Dictate formats numbers, currency, phone numbers, dates, times, and addresses based on settings in its Auto Formatting dialog. You can modify these settings as discussed in the section titled "Setting Auto Formatting Options" on page 42.

To dictate currency amounts:

In Dictation mode, say the currency amount, using the appropriate command for the currency symbol in Table 3.13.

Table 3.14 shows some examples of how you can dictate a variety of currency amounts.

To dictate telephone numbers:

In Dictation mode, say each digit of the phone number.

Dictate types each number you say. When it types the last number, it formats the number as a phone number. Table 3.15 shows some examples of what you can say and how Dictate types it.

TIP This works for U.S. phone numbers. For phone numbers with different formatting, you need to dictate any punctuation necessary.

To dictate dates:

In Dictation mode, do one of the following:

- Say the date as you normally would.
- Say the date with specific formatting or punctuation.

Table 3.16 shows some examples of how Dictate types what you say.

To dictate times:

In Dictation mode, say the time the way you want it formatted.

Table 3.17 shows some examples of how Dictate types what you say.

TIP To make sure a time is formatted as a time, say *A M* or *P M* after the time. Otherwise, it may be typed as a regular number.

TABLE 3.15 Phone Number Dictation Examples

When you say this:	Dictate types this:
Two One Two Six Two Three One Two Three Four	212-623-1234
One Eight Hundred Five Five Five One Two One Two	1-800-555-1212
Two Oh One Five Six Seven Five Oh Eight Seven Extension Ten	201-567-5087 extension 10

TABLE 3.16 Date Dictation Examples

When you say this:	Dictate types this:
March Fifteenth	March 15
June Thirtieth Nineteen Sixty One	June 30, 1961
Thursday September Fifteenth Two Thousand Eleven	Thursday, September 15, 2011
Six Slash Three Zero Slash Six One or *Six Slash Thirty Slash Sixty One*	6/30/61
Fifteen September Two Thousand Eleven	15 September 2011
The Nineteen Nineties	the 1990s
The Nineteen Ninety Apostrophe S	the 1990's

TABLE 3.17 Time Dictation Examples

When you say this:	Dictate types this:
Ten Oh Clock	10 o'clock
Ten A M	10 AM
Ten Oh Clock A M	10:00 AM
Ten Fifty Two P M	10:52 PM
Fifteen Thirty Zulu	1530 Z

To dictate addresses with Zip codes:

In Dictation mode, say the complete address, speaking each part of the address as a phrase followed by a pause:

- Number and street
- City and state
- Each digit of the Zip code

Table 3.18 shows some examples.

TIP Note that when you dictate addresses, Dictate may write out the name of the state. But when you say the digits of the Zip code, the state name is replaced with the official two-character postal service abbreviation.

TABLE 3.18 Address Dictation Examples

When you say this:	Dictate types this:
One Twenty Three Main Street [pause] *Wickenburg Arizona* [pause] *Eight Five Three Nine Zero*	123 Main St., Wickenburg, AZ 85390
Sixteen Dash Forty Three One Hundred and Twenty Third Avenue [pause] *Bayside New York* [pause] *One One Two Three Four*	16–43 123rd Ave., Bayside, NY 11234
Ten Oak Street Apartment Six B [pause] *Quincy Washington* [pause] *Nine Eight Eight Four Eight*	10 Oak St., Apt. 6 B Quincy, WA 98848

Setting Auto Formatting Options

The way numbers, addresses, phone numbers, dates, times, and other special text is automatically formatted by Dictate is based, in part, on settings in the Auto Formatting dialog.

You can review these settings to get a better idea of how Dictate formats what you say. You can also change these settings to fine-tune them for your own needs.

To open the Auto Formatting dialog:

Choose Tools > Auto Formatting.

The Auto Formatting dialog appears **A**.

To set Addresses automatic formatting options:

Toggle check boxes in the Addresses area of the Auto Formatting dialog **A** to enable or disable automatic formatting for various address components:

- **Street addresses** formats postal addresses with a comma after the street, city, and state. It also converts spoken state names to two-character abbreviations. Table 3.18 shows some examples.

- **UK and Canadian postcodes** formats six-character postal codes with a space in the middle. To dictate these postal codes, just say each character.

- **Web and email addresses** formats URLs and email addresses as they would normally be typed, without extra spaces.

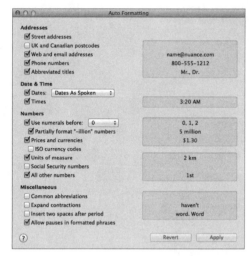

A The default settings in the Auto Formatting dialog.

✓ **Dates As Spoken**
  January 5, 2011
  January 05, 2011
  Jan 5, 2011
  Jan 05, 2011
  1/5/2011
  1/5/11
  01/05/2011
  01/05/11
  01-05-11
  5 January, 2011
  5/1/2011
  5/1/11
  05/01/2011
  05/01/11
  05-Jan-11

B Choosing an option other than Dates As Spoken from this pop-up menu forces Dictate to use a specific date format when typing the dates you say.

- **Phone numbers** formats seven- or ten-digit number strings, as well as 11-digit numbers beginning with a 1, as hyphenated phone numbers. Table 3.15 shows some examples.

TIP Dictate does not recognize "vanity" phone numbers, such as 800-DICTATE. To type these numbers, spell them out with punctuation.

- **Abbreviated titles** types courtesy title words such as *Doctor*, *Mister*, or *Reverend* to *Dr.*, *Mr.*, or *Rev.*

To set Date & Time automatic formatting options:

Toggle check boxes and choose a pop-up menu option in the Date & Time area of the Auto Formatting dialog **A** to set how dates and times are automatically formatted:

- **Dates** formats spoken dates either as spoken (Table 3.16) or using a predefined format. With this check box turned on, you can choose a desired format from the pop-up menu **B**.

- **Times** formats spoken times as times. To display the time in a specific format, be sure to dictate it that way. Refer to Table 3.17 for examples.

To set Numbers automatic formatting options:

Toggle check boxes and choose a pop-up menu option in the Numbers area of the Auto Formatting dialog Ⓐ to set how numbers are formatted:

- **Use numerals before** enables you to choose a value from a pop-up menu Ⓒ to set a cut-off point for where Dictate should enter numerals instead of words for spoken numbers. With this check box turned on, any number before the number you choose is written as text and any number after it is entered as a numeral. For example, if you chose 10 from the menu, when you say *Five*, it's written as **five** and when you say *Fifteen*, it's written as *15*.

- **Partially format "-illion" numbers** works in Dictation mode to format numbers in the millions, billions, and so on, with a numeral and the word. With this option turned on, for example, saying *Twelve Million* types the number as *12 million*. To use this formatting, the **Use numerals before** option must be turned on.

TIP In Numbers mode, saying Twelve Million types 12,000,000, no matter how this is set.

- **Prices and currencies** formats currency amounts as shown in Table 3.14.

- **ISO currency codes** types ISO currency abbreviations (Table 3.19) instead of currency symbols. To use this formatting, the **Prices and currencies** option must be turned on.

- **Units of measure** formats measurements with symbols and abbreviations. For example, saying *Five Feet Eight Inches* types *5'8"* and saying *Sixteen Grams* types *16 g*.

| ✓ 0 |
| 2 |
| 10 |
| 100 |

Ⓒ Any number before the number you choose will be typed as a word instead of a numeral.

TABLE 3.19 ISO Currency Codes

Currency Name	Symbol	ISO Code
U S Dollar	$	USD
Canadian Dollar	C$	CAD
Euro	€	EUR
Yen	¥	JPY
British Pound	£	GBP
Swiss Franc	F	CHF

- **Social Security numbers** formats nine-digit numbers as U.S. Social Security numbers with dashes.

- **All other numbers** formats other kinds of numbers as spoken. This enables the ability to dictate Roman numerals (refer to the section titled "To dictate Roman numerals" on page 38), include decimal points in numbers, and enter negative numbers.

To set Miscellaneous automatic formatting options:

Toggle check boxes in the Miscellaneous area of the Auto Formatting dialog **Ⓐ** to turn other automatic formatting options on or off:

- **Common abbreviations** types words that have commonly used abbreviations using those abbreviations. For example, if you say *Mister Smith*, Dictate types *Mr. Smith*.

- **Expand contractions** types out contractions as full words. For example, if you say *haven't*, Dictate types *have not*.

TIP Dictate only expands contractions if the contraction can only be interpreted one way. For example, if you say *She's many things*, Dictate will not expand *She's* because it could be *She is* or *She has*.

- **Insert two spaces after period** inserts two spaces instead of only one after a period.

- **Allow pauses in formatted phrases** allows Dictate's auto formatting features to work even if you pause while speaking a phrase that should be auto formatted, such as an address or phone number.

To save Auto Formatting settings:

1. Click the Apply button in the bottom of the Auto Formatting dialog **A**.

2. A confirmation dialog appears **D**. It warns you that Dictate will reload the profile and disable correction on any previously dictated text. Click OK.

3. Wait while Dictate reloads your profile. When it is finished, you can continue working with Dictate.

TIP You can always edit text with Dictate, even after saving changes to Auto Formatting options as discussed here. Simply activate the document you want to edit and say *Cache Document*. Dictate reads all text back into memory so you can use Dictate with that document again.

TIP As you probably guessed, Auto Formatting settings are profile specific. Changes for one profile do not affect any others. You can learn more about profiles in Chapter 1.

D You'll need to click OK in this dialog to save Auto Formatting settings and reload your profile.

Editing Text

Entering text into a document is the first—and arguably the most important—part of creating a text-based document. But unless you know exactly what you want to say and how to say it as you dictate, you'll likely need to edit the original text to make changes in content and formatting.

Dragon Dictate can help you do that, too. You can use voice commands to move the insertion point to various places within your document and insert text. You can select, replace, and delete text. You can also use voice commands to change capitalization and add punctuation, such as quotes or brackets, around text. You can even tell Dictate to help you proofread a document by reading it back to you.

This chapter covers all of these topics. But it begins with some information that's vital to prevent frustration when working with Dictate to edit documents: the so-called "Golden Rule."

In This Chapter

The Golden Rule

As you dictate to transcribe text with Dragon Dictate, Dictate creates and maintains a record of what it has typed for you. This record, called a *cache*, is relied upon by Dictate when you use commands to navigate, select, and edit text.

If you manually enter or edit text in a document, Dictate doesn't know anything about these changes. Because of this, Dictate can't reliably react to commands to navigate within manually entered or modified text. So if you issue a voice command to select or modify certain text after manually changing a document, there's a chance that Dictate might not respond as you expect.

And that brings up what Nuance Communications, makers of Dragon Dictate, refer to as "The Golden Rule": "When you're working with text, don't mix your voice with your hands."

Here's an example. Suppose you used dictation to type the phrase. *I'm thrilled that my computer can take dictation for me* **A**. You decide that you want to replace the word thrilled with something less emphatic, like *happy*. So you say **Select thrilled**. **Happy**. Dictate selects the word *thrilled* and replaces it with the word *happy*, leaving the blinking insertion point right after *happy* **B**.

Now you want to continue typing from the end. But because you're so excited that your computer can take dictation—you really *are* thrilled, you see—you forget the Golden Rule and click at the end of the document **C** instead of using the **Go to End** command. From that point forward, Dictate is out of sync with what's in the document window.

I'm thrilled that my computer can take dictation for me.

A In this example, I've dictated some text,...

I'm happy that my computer can take dictation for me.

B ... and then used a voice command to select and replace a word.

I'm happy that my computer can take dictation for me.

C But then I violated the Golden Rule by clicking at the end of the sentence instead of using a voice command to get there.

I'm happy that my computer can take dictation for me.

D Subsequently issuing another voice command such as **Select previous three words** results in an incorrect selection.

Why did that simple click confuse Dictate? Because *you* moved the insertion point and Dictate has no way of knowing that you did. As a result, if you then say, for example, **Select previous three words**, Dictate will not really know what the previous three words are and may select the wrong text **D**. It's all downhill from there.

There are exceptions to the Golden Rule. Because Note Pad is part of Dictate, Dictate can see what's in the Note Pad window. In most cases, it can still figure out what you want to do, even if you mixed voice and keyboard editing.

Dictate also allows you to mix voice and keyboard editing for TextEdit and Microsoft Word. To do so, however, you must properly set the Auto Cache option in the Dictation pane of Dictate preferences.

TIP You must have Dictate version 2.5 or later to mix voice and keyboard editing successfully with Microsoft Word.

If you unintentionally or unavoidably violate the Golden Rule—for example, you manually edit part of a document that you can't seem to edit using voice commands—you can instruct Dictate to read and re-cache the document. This throws out everything Dictate knows about the document—including your recorded voice—and stores a new version of it in cache. You can then continue working on it using voice commands.

This part of the chapter explains how to set up TextEdit and Word so that you don't need to follow the Golden Rule as well as how to clear the cache in case you do violate it when you shouldn't.

To set up Auto Cache for TextEdit & Microsoft Word:

1. In Dragon Dictate, choose Dictate > Preferences, or press Command-Comma.

2. Click the Dictation button at the top of the window that appears **Ⓐ**.

3. Turn on the check boxes for each application you plan to mix dictation and keyboard editing.

4. Click the window's close button.

TIP If documents for either application are open, close and reopen them to cache their contents.

To rebuild the cache for a document:

In Dictation or Command mode, use one of the following techniques:

- Say *Cache Document*. This clears out the cache and reads the entire document back into cache so Dictate knows what the document contains.

- Select the text you want to cache and say *Cache Selection*. This clears out the cache and reads the selected text back into the cache so Dictate knows what it contains. If you want to work with another part of the document, you need to cache that.

- Say *Purge Cache*. This clears out the cache, thus telling Dictate that the document is empty. In some cases—for example, when working with an automatically cached document, such as Note Pad, TextEdit, or Word—the cache is automatically resaved.

TIP It's a good idea to cache a document any time Dictate reacts unexpectedly to voice commands.

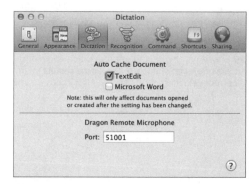

Ⓔ By default, Auto Cache is turned on for TextEdit but turned off for Microsoft Word. To mix voice and keyboard editing in an application, turn its check box on.

TABLE 4.1 Dictation Reversal Commands

To do this:	Say this:
Delete the last word you dictated	*Scratch Word* or *Delete Word*
Delete the last phrase you dictated	*Scratch That* or *Delete That*
Undo your last dictation or edit	*Undo Dictation*
Undo the undo command	*Redo Dictation*

Undoing Dictation

As you dictate text and make changes to existing text in a document, you may change your mind or want to immediately remove an error before continuing. There are a number of commands you can use to do this (Table 4.1).

TIP The *Undo Dictation* command is an all-purpose Undo command while working with Dictate to dictate and edit text.

TIP You can use these commands repeatedly to delete previous words or phrases or undo previous actions.

To delete the last word you dictated:

Say *Scratch Word* or *Delete Word*.

The last word you dictated is removed.

TIP If the last "word" dictated is actually punctuation—for example, a period—that punctuation is deleted.

To delete the last phrase you dictated:

Say *Scratch That* or *Delete That*.

The last phrase you dictated is removed.

TIP Dictate determines what a "phrase" is based on pauses you made when you dictated.

To undo your last dictated action:

Say *Undo Dictation*.

What happens depends on what you last dictated:

- If the last thing you did was dictate text, the last phrase dictated is deleted.

- If the last thing you did was issue a text editing command, that command is reversed.

Navigating within a Document

Moving the blinking insertion point within a document window enables you to insert text in a specific place. As required by the Golden Rule (page 48), you should use voice commands to move the insertion point. There are a number of commands you can use in Dictation mode to get the job done (Table 4.2):

- **Go To** and **Move To** commands move the insertion point to the beginning or end of the document.

- **Move** commands move the insertion point a specified number of words, from 1 to 99.

- **Insert** commands move the insertion point before or after a specific word or phrase.

- **Arrow** commands move the insertion point right, left, up, or down one character or line at a time. (These commands work in Dictation and Command modes.)

To move the insertion point:

In Dictation mode, say the appropriate command (Table 4.2). The insertion point moves accordingly:

- When you move to a location after a word or phrase, the insertion point appears right after that word or the last word in the phrase **Ⓐ**.

- When you move to a location before a word or phrase, the insertion point appears right before the space preceding that word or the first word in the phrase **Ⓑ**—unless there is no space before it.

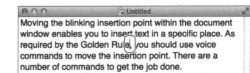

ⒶⒷ In the top example, I said *Insert After Golden Rule*; in the bottom example, I said *Insert Before Golden Rule*. Note where the insertion point appears in relation to spaces.

TABLE 4.2 Navigation Commands

To move the insertion point here:	Say this:
The beginning of the document	*Go To Beginning* or *Move To Beginning Of Document*
The end of the document	*Go To End* or *Move To End Of Document*
The number of words backward that you specify	*Move Backwards* n *Words*
The number of words forward that you specify	*Move Forwards* n *Words*
Before a specific word	*Insert Before* word
After a specific word	*Insert After* word
Before a specific phrase	*Insert Before* firstword *Through* lastword or *Insert Before* firstword *To* lastword
After a specific phrase	*Insert After* firstword *Through* lastword or *Insert After* firstword *To* lastword
One character right	**Right Arrow**
One character left	**Left Arrow**
One line up	**Up Arrow**
One line down	**Down Arrow**

Selecting Text

You select text to make changes to it. While it's tempting to select text with your mouse, the Golden Rule (page 48) requires that you use voice commands instead. There are a number of Select commands you can use in Dictation mode to select text in a document (Table 4.3).

TIP If a word or phrase appears multiple times in a document, Dictate selects the text closest to the insertion point. You can use navigation commands (page 51) to position the insertion point closer to the text you want to select before using the Select command.

TIP The *Select Next* and *Select Previous* commands will not work if text is already selected. If necessary, use a navigation command (page 51) to position the insertion point before using one of these commands.

TIP If the word *all* exists in the document, the *Select All* command will select that word. Say *Select the Document* instead.

To select text:

In Dictation mode, say the appropriate command (Table 4.3). The text is selected accordingly **A** **B** **C**.

A Immediately after dictating this text, I said *Select changes*, …

B …then *Select use To instead*, …

C … and then *Select the Previous Three Words*.

TABLE 4.3 Selection Commands

To select this:	Say this:
A specific word	*Select* word
A specific phrase	*Select* firstword *Through* lastword or *Select* firstword *To* lastword
The next word	*Select Next*
The previous word	*Select Previous*
The number of words forward that you specify	*Select the Next* n *Words*
The number of words backward that you specify	*Select the Previous* n *Words*
Select all the text in the document	*Select All* or *Select The Document*

Modifying Text

In addition to using a Select command (page 53) to select text and then saying new text to replace it with, there are a number of other commands you can use to modify text with Dragon Dictate (Table 4.4):

- **Delete** commands delete text you specify.

- **Capitalize** commands change the text you specify to title case.

- **Lowercase** commands change the text you specify to all lowercase letters.

- **Uppercase** commands change the text you specify to all uppercase letters.

TIP If a word or phrase appears multiple times in a document, Dictate performs the command on the text closest to the insertion point. You can use navigation commands (page 51) to position the insertion point closer to the text you want to edit before using the editing command.

To replace text:

1. Use a Select command (Table 4.3) to select the text you want to change **A**.

2. Say the new text.

   The selected text is replaced with what you said **B**.

To delete or change the case of text:

Use one of the text modification commands (Table 4.4) to make changes as desired to the text you specify.

Once you have typed text, you can use voice commands to modify it. For example, you can select a word and then say a new word to replace it.

A In this example, I said *Select new*...

Once you have typed text, you can use voice commands to modify it. For example, you can select a word and then say a different word to replace it.

B ... and then said *different* to replace *new* with *different*.

TABLE 4.4 Modification Commands

To make this change:	Say this:
Delete a specific word	*Delete* word
Delete a specific phrase	*Delete* firstword *Through* lastword or *Delete* firstword *To* lastword
Delete selected text	*Delete Selection*
Change a specific word to title case	*Capitalize* word
Change a specific phrase to title case	*Capitalize* firstword *Through* lastword or *Capitalize* firstword *To* lastword
Change selected text to title case	*Capitalize Selection*
Change a specific word to all lowercase letters	*Lowercase* word
Change a specific phrase to all lowercase letters	*Lowercase* firstword *Through* lastword or *Lowercase* firstword *To* lastword
Change selected text to all lowercase letters	*Lowercase Selection*
Change a specific word to all uppercase letters	*Uppercase* word
Change a specific phrase to all uppercase letters	*Uppercase* firstword *Through* lastword or *Uppercase* firstword *To* lastword
Change selected text to all uppercase letters	*Uppercase Selection*

Adding Punctuation to Existing Text

Dragon Dictate's Surround the Word feature enables you to insert certain types of punctuation around text that has already been typed. All you do is issue a command that includes the type of punctuation you want with the word or phrase you want to punctuate. You can use this feature to surround text with quotes (double, single, straight, or smart), parentheses, brackets (square, curly, or angle), and Spanish punctuation (question marks and exclamation marks).

A complete table of the command possibilities would be too lengthy to include in this book. Instead, consult Table 4.5 for guidance on how to construct a valid Surround the Word command. Just take one component from each column to build your command.

TIP To better understand what symbols each punctuation command produces, consult Table 3.4 (page 31).

TABLE 4.5 Commands for Inserting Punctuation Around Words

Start by saying this:	Say one of these punctuation commands:	Then say this:	And then say one of these commands to specify the text to be punctuated:
Put	*Single Quotes*	*Around*	*The Selection*
	Quotes or *Double Quotes*		word
	Single Straight Quotes		*The Word* word
	Straight Quotes or *Double Straight Quotes*		*The Words* firstword *Through* lastword
			The Words firstword *To* lastword
	Parentheses		
	Brackets		
	Braces or *Curly Brackets*		
	Angle Brackets		
	Spanish Question Marks		
	Spanish Exclamation Marks		

To add punctuation to selected text:

1. Use a Select command (Table 4.3) to select the text you want to punctuate **A**.

2. Say a command in the format *Put* **punctuation type** *Around The Selection* (Table 4.5).

   The punctuation you specified is inserted around the selected text **B**.

To add punctuation to existing text:

Say a command in the format *Put* **punctuation type** *Around* **specified words** (Table 4.5).

The punctuation type you specified is inserted around the text you specified **C**.

TIP If you can't get Dictate to surround the exact text you want punctuated, try using a navigation command (Table 4.2) to move the insertion point and then insert individual punctuation characters listed in Table 3.4 (page 31).

A In this example, I said *Select Surround the Word* to select some text ...

B ... and then said *Put Quotes Around the Selection* to put double quotes around the selected text.

C In this example I said *Put Brackets Around Spanish* and then said *Put Parentheses Around or phrase*.

Dragon Dictate's proofreading feature makes it possible for Dictate to read your text back to you. You'll find that Dictate not only reads back your words, but it includes the appropriate pauses signaled by the punctuation in your text. You might find this feature helpful for catching errors that are easily overlooked when you read text back to yourself. Table 4.6 lists the commands that work with this feature; you can substitute the command Proofread for Read in any command.

Ⓐ Dictate selects each word it reads.

TABLE 4.6 Proofreading Commands

To do this:	Say this:
Read the entire document	*Read Document*
Read selected text	*Read Selection*
Read specific text	*Read The Words* firstword *Through* lastword or *Read the Words* firstword *To* lastword
Stop reading	*Stop Reading*

Proofreading Text

Dragon Dictate's proofreading feature makes it possible for Dictate to read your text back to you. You'll find that Dictate not only reads back your words, but includes the appropriate pauses signaled by the punctuation in your text. You might find this feature helpful for catching errors that are easily overlooked when you read text back to yourself. Table 4.6 lists the commands that work with this feature; you can substitute the command *Proofread* for *Read* in any command.

Dictate uses the Text to Speech feature and voices of Mac OS X to read back text. The voices, although obviously synthetic, are remarkably clear and easy to understand. You can change the default voice and reading speed by setting options in Mac OS X's Speech preferences pane.

TIP Dictate's Proofreading feature works in Dictation mode.

TIP When Dictate begins reading, it may switch to Sleep mode. It will return to Dictation mode when it is finished reading.

To read back the entire document:

Say *Read Document* or *Proofread Document*.

Dictate reads the document aloud, starting from the beginning, highlighting each word as it reads Ⓐ. It continues until you stop it or it reaches the end of the document.

TIP If Dictate wants to type *read document* instead of actually reading the document, try saying *Read The Document*.

To read selected text:

1. Use a Select command (Table 4.3) to select the text you want Dictate to read 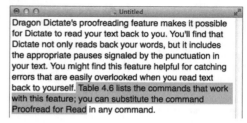.

2. Say *Read Selection*.

Dictate reads the selected text aloud, starting from the beginning of the selection. It continues until you stop it or it reaches the end of the selected text.

To stop reading:

1. If necessary, say *Wake Up*.

2. Say *Stop Reading*.

To change the proofreading voice:

1. Choose Apple > System Preferences to open the System Preferences window.

2. Click the Speech icon.

3. In the Speech preferences pane, click the Text to Speech button to show its options .

4. Choose a different voice from the System Voice pop-up menu **D**.

5. If desired, use the Speaking Rate slider to change the speech speed.

6. To hear what the voice will sound like, click Play.

7. Repeat step 4 through 6 as desired to set a voice and speed you like.

8. Close the Speech preferences pane.

   The voice you selected will be used from that point forward by Dictate's proofreading feature.

TIP You can add voices to the System Voice menu. In Step 4, choose Customize to display a dialog with additional voice options **E**. Turn on the check box beside each voice you want to add to the menu and click OK.

B In this example, I said *Select Table Four Point Six Through Read* to select text to be read to me.

C The Text to Speech options of the Speech preferences pane.

D Choose a voice from the System Voice pop-up menu

E Use this dialog to specify which voices should appear on the System Voice menu.

Fine-Tuning Speech Recognition

Dragon Dictate's speech recognition capabilities are *very* good—especially if you're able to speak clearly into a reasonably good quality microphone in a relatively quiet place.

But it's not perfect. Sometimes Dictate won't hear you quite right and type a word or phrase you didn't actually say. Often, you can improve Dictate's ability to understand your dictation by doing additional voice training, as discussed in Chapter 1.

Other times, Dictate won't type the right word or phrase because it simply *doesn't know* what you said—perhaps because you used an unusual proper noun or a technical term. Or maybe it heard the right word but didn't spell it the way you need it spelled—you were referring to *Mr. Jonson* and Dictate typed *Mr. Johnson*.

This chapter explores four ways to fine-tune Dictate's speech recognition capabilities to better suit your needs: using the Recognition window, doing vocabulary training, editing Dictate's vocabulary, and sharing vocabulary lists between profiles.

In This Chapter

Using the Recognition Window

The Recognition window, which was discussed briefly in Chapter 2, is a tool within Dragon Dictate that enables you to tell Dictate about errors it made in interpreting what you said.

When you open the Recognition window, it floats over all other windows so it's always visible. Then, as you dictate, it lists the phrases you're most likely to have said ⓐ. The phrase it actually typed is the first one in the list. But if it typed the wrong thing and the right thing appears in the list, you can tell Dictate what you *really* said. This is referred to as *Training the Voice Model*, and it's an important part of getting Dictate to work best for you.

Using the Recognition window to train Dictate to understand your voice only works with documents that you have dictated and only if the recording of your dictation is still available. If you typed a document or used the **Cache Document** command to re-read a document that you dictated, Dictate will not have a recording of your voice. Because of that, it will have nothing to interpret. It can't offer options and, even if it could, it couldn't compare options to the sound of your voice speaking the words.

You can train Dictate with the Recognition window in two different ways:

- Correct what you just dictated.
- Select and correct something previously dictated.

This part of the chapter looks at how you can use the Recognition window to train Dictate to better understand your voice.

ⓐ The Recognition window enables you to correct Dictate when it gets something wrong.

Phrases, Utterances, & the Recognition Window

Throughout this book, I generally refer to bits of dictated text between pauses as *phrases*. Dictate thinks of these as *utterances*.

As you work with Dictate, you may notice that it transcribes what you say one phrase (or utterance) at a time. This is because Dictate evaluates what you say by utterance.

It makes sense, then, that the Recognition window should work on utterances. Indeed, you'll see complete phrases, as you dictated them, in the Recognition window.

Even when you go back and train Dictate using the Recognition window, telling it exactly the source text it should use for training, it may display the actual utterance. This can be longer or shorter than the text you specified.

B One way to open the Recognition window is to click the Recognition button in the Status window.

To display the Recognition window:

Use one of the following techniques:

- Say **Show Recognition Window**.
- Click the Recognition button in the Status window **B**.
- Press the Command-F9.
- Use a **Train** command. (Refer to Table 5.1 and the section titled "To correct previously dictated text" on page 62 for more information.)

The Recognition window opens. If the insertion point is after or in text in the document window that can be used for training, a list of options appears **A**.

TIP You can set an option in Dictate's Recognition preferences to automatically open the Recognition window when you are in Dictation or Spelling mode as soon as the insertion point is within or after a dictated phrase. Learn how in the section titled "Recognition Preferences" on page 136.

To close the Recognition window:

Use one of the following techniques:

- Say one of the following:
  - ▸ **Hide Recognition Window**
  - ▸ **Cancel Training**
  - ▸ **Cancel Recognition**
- Click the Recognition window's close button.
- Press Command-F9.

TIP By default, an option in Dictate's Recognition preferences window is set to automatically close the Recognition window after you use it to replace a phrase. Learn how to change this option in the section titled "Recognition Preferences" on page 136.

To correct what you just dictated:

1. If the Recognition window is not displayed, show it.

2. Dictate as usual.

3. After each phrase, check the text in your document and in the Recognition window.

4. If the text in the document is not correct, do one of the following:

   ▸ If the correct text appears in the Recognition window 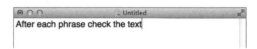, say **Pick** or **Choose** followed by the number of the correct choice. Dictate replaces the incorrect phrase with the phrase you selected 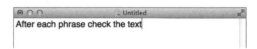.

   ▸ If the correct text does not appear in the Recognition window say **Undo Dictation** and try dictating that text again or edit the closest alternative as discussed in the section titled "To edit an alternative" on page 64 and choose that.

5. Continue dictating, following steps 2 through 4 until finished.

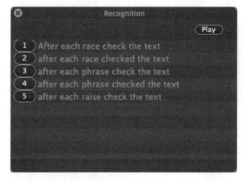

C In this example, Dictate misheard me. I really said what's in the third line.

D When I said **Pick Three**, Dictate replaced the incorrect text with the text I chose.

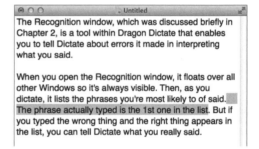

E This is what DIctate selected when I said, **Train The Words The phrase actually typed**.

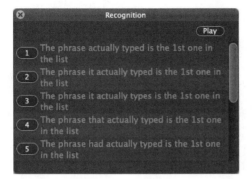

F What I really said was the second option on this list.

The Recognition window, which was discussed briefly in Chapter 2, is a tool within Dragon Dictate that enables you to tell Dictate about errors it made in interpreting what you said.

When you open the Recognition window, it floats over all other Windows so it's always visible. Then, as you dictate, it lists the phrases you're most likely to of said. The phrase it actually typed is the 1st one in the list. But if you typed the wrong thing and the right thing appears in the list, you can tell Dictate what you really said.

G Dictate replaces the selected text with my choice from the Recognition window.

TABLE 5.1 Speech Recognition Training Commands

To Select This For Training:	Say This:
A single word	**Train The Word** word
A series of words	**Train The Words** phrase or
	Train The Words firstword **Through** lastword or
	Train The Words firstword **To** lastword

To correct previously dictated text:

1. If the Recognition window is not displayed, show it.

2. Use one of the **Train** commands (Table 5.1) to select incorrectly typed text to train **E**.

TIP Remember: Dictate selects text for training by utterance, so it might not select exactly the text you told it to.

3. Compare the text in the document to the options in the Recognition window **F**.

4. Do one of the following:
   - ▸ If the correct option is displayed, say Pick or Choose followed by the number of the correct choice. Dictate replaces the incorrect phrase with the phrase you selected **G**.
   - ▸ If the correct option is not displayed, you can either repeat the selected text that Dictate should have typed to replace it or edit the closest alternative as discussed in the section titled "To edit an alternative" on page 64 and choose that.

TIP If you look closely, you can see that the text in the document window has other errors. For example, the sentence immediately before the highlighted one ends with "most likely to of said." I know I said *have* rather than *of*, but Dictate heard *of* and only offers that in its Recognition window suggestions. I could fix it manually by saying *Select of* and then saying— more clearly, of course—*have*. Or I can edit an alternative as discussed in on the next page.

To edit an alternative:

1. In the Recognition window, identify the number of the alternative that is closest to what you really said.

2. Say **Edit** followed by the alternative number. For example, if alternative number 1 was closest, say **Edit 1**.

   An edit box appears around the alternative you selected .

3. Edit the selected text so it is correct . You can edit by speaking in Dictation or Spelling mode or by typing the correct text into the edit box.

4. When the text is correct, say **Pick** or **Choose** followed by the number of the alternative you edited; for example, **Pick 1**.

   The revised text replaces the selected text in your document 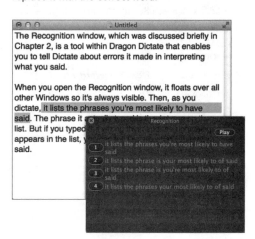.

TIP To cancel the edit without changing your document, say *Cancel Edit*.

To play back the recording for a phrase:

With phrases listed in the Recognition window ❶, do one of the following:

- Say **Play the Selection**.
- Click the Play button in the Recognition window.

Dictate plays back the utterance that resulted in the text in the recognition window so you can hear what you said and what Dictate is interpreting.

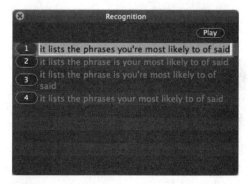

❶ Saying **Edit 1** selects the first alternative for editing.

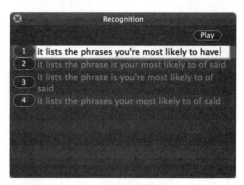

❶ In this example, I said **Select of** to select the incorrect word and then clearly said **have** to replace it with the correct word.

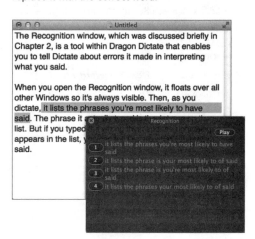

❶ I then said **Pick 1** to save my edit and apply it to the selected text in my document.

A The Vocabulary Training window.

B The Tools menu offers two commands for working with the Vocabulary Training window.

Adding Words with Vocabulary Training

Dragon Dictate has a huge built-in vocabulary of more than 150,000 words. Not only does this vocabulary include words you'd expect to find in most magazine articles or books, but it also includes many abbreviations, acronyms, and proper nouns.

Despite this, it's not uncommon to need to dictate words or phrases that Dictate simply doesn't know. These could be technical terms, jargon, or proper nouns that you use in your documents. Or they could simply be unusual spellings of names that Dictate spells a different way.

Chances are, you already have these special words in a document. Maybe they're in a report or letter you wrote with Microsoft Word or a memo you wrote with Text-Edit. You can "feed" that text to Dictate's Vocabulary Training window **A** and add unknown words to Dictate. Here's how.

TIP Because Dictate's processing needs to review words in context, only use this feature with text that appears in sentences or paragraphs. Adding lists of words may affect Dictate's ability to use the correct word.

To open the Vocabulary Training window:

Use one of the following techniques:

- Say **Activate Vocabulary Training Window** or **Show Vocabulary Training Window**.

- Choose Tools > Vocabulary Training **B**.

- Use a **Train** command. (Refer to the section titled "To add selected text to the vocabulary training window" on page 67 for more information.)

To close the Vocabulary Training window:

Use one of the following techniques:

- Say *Hide Vocabulary Training Window*.
- Click the Vocabulary Training Window's close button **A**.

To add text files to the Vocabulary Training window:

1. Use one of the following techniques to add entire files to the file list in the Vocabulary Training window:

   ▸ Drag a document file from a Finder window into the file list **C**.

   ▸ Click the Add button beneath the file list and then use the standard Open dialog that appears to locate and select the file **D**. Click Open.

   TIP Dictate can open files in plain text, RTF, DOC, or ODT formats.

   The file appears in the list **E**.

2. Repeat this process to add as many files as you like.

3. Click the right arrow button at the bottom of the Vocabulary Training window to begin processing the contents of the document.

4. Continue following the steps in the section titled "To complete vocabulary training" on page 67.

   TIP By adding multiple files to the Vocabulary Training window, Dictate can scan all words in all files at once, speeding up the process of adding words to Dictate's vocabulary.

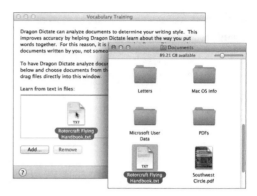

C You can drag a compatible file from a Finder window to the Vocabulary Training window.

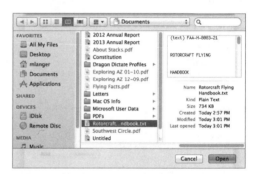

D You can also add a file to the Vocabulary Training window using a standard Open dialog.

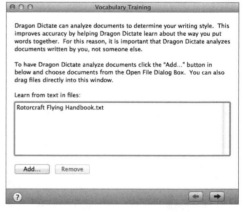

E The file you added appears in the list.

All the words in the text supplied are already in this vocabulary. Vocabulary Training may still get valuable information about the frequency and order of the words.

F If Dictate already knows all the words, it tells you.

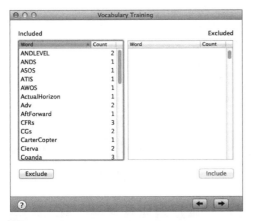

G Dictate assumes you want to add all the unknown words to its vocabulary. My source document, however, is full of word fragments and other undesirable text.

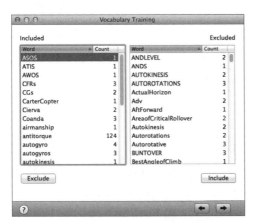

H Fortunately, you can specify which words should be excluded from the vocabulary.

To add selected text to the Vocabulary Training window:

1. Use one of the following techniques to add selected text to the file list in the Vocabulary Training window:

   ▸ In any document window, select the text you want to add and say *Train Vocabulary From Selection*.

   ▸ In a Note Pad window, select the text you want to add and choose Tools > Train Vocabulary from Selection **B**.

   Dictate begins processing the contents of the selection.

2. Continue following the steps in the section titled "To complete vocabulary training" on page 67.

To complete vocabulary training:

1. Follow the steps in one of the previous two sections.

2. One of two things happens:

   ▸ If Dictate already knows all the words, it displays a message telling you **F**. Click the right arrow button at the bottom of the window.

   ▸ If Dictate found unknown words, it displays them in a list on the left side of the window **G**. To exclude a word, select it in the list and then click the Exclude button to move it to the list on the right **H**. Repeat this process for all words you don't want to add. When you have finished excluding words, click the right arrow button.

3. Wait while Dictate processes the text. If necessary, it adds words to its vocabulary. When it's finished, it tells you.

4. Click Done to close the Vocabulary Training window.

Editing Dictate's Vocabulary

Another way to add words to Dragon Dictate's vocabulary is to manually enter them into the Vocabulary Editor window. This window lists the over 150,000 words in Dictate's vocabulary  plus the ones you add manually or through Vocabulary Training (page 65) **B**.

The Vocabulary Editor window goes a step farther, though. It lets you remove words you don't want Dictate to type at all. This means that you can replace a word spelled one way with the same word spelled another way. This can come in very handy when you have a client who spells his name oddly or your publisher's new style guide prefers *email* instead of *e-mail*.

This part of the chapter explains how you can open, review, add words to, and remove words from the Vocabulary Editor window.

A The Vocabulary Editor window, displaying the Built-In vocabulary...

To open the Vocabulary Editor window:

Use one of the following techniques:

- Say *Access Vocabulary Editor Window* or *Show Vocabulary Editor Window*.

- Choose Tools > Vocabulary Editor, or press Shift-Command-V.

To close the Vocabulary Editor window:

Use one of the following techniques:

- Say *Hide Vocabulary Editor Window*.

- Click the Vocabulary Editor window's close button.

B ... and the user-added vocabulary.

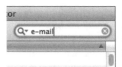

C Enter all or part of the text you want to find in the search field.

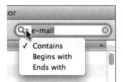

D If desired, use the pop-up menu to tell Dictate where to search.

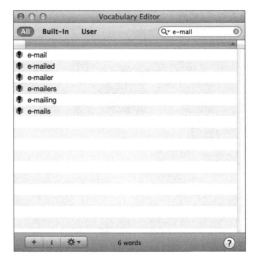

E If Dictate finds matches, it lists them in the window.

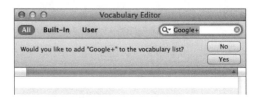

F If Dictate doesn't find any matches, it offers to create a new entry for you.

To see a specific vocabulary list:

Click a buttons at the top of the window:

- **All** shows all vocabulary entries.
- **Built-In A** shows the vocabulary words that come with Dictate.
- **User B** shows the vocabulary words you added.

To search for a vocabulary entry:

1. In the Vocabulary Editor window, click the button for the list you want to search **A B**.

TIP If you're not sure whether an entry will be in the Built-In list or User list, click All.

2. Click in the search field at the top of the window to position the insertion point.
3. Type the word or part of the word you are looking for **C**.
4. Click the menu button on the left end of the search field and choose an option **D**:
   - **Contains** matches the text anywhere in an entry.
   - **Begins with** matches the text when it occurs at the beginning of an entry.
   - **Ends with** matches the text when it occurs at the end of an entry.

TIP Dictate searches both the written and spoken forms of the entry; learn more in "To set vocabulary word options" on page 70.

5. Press Return or Enter.
6. Wait while Dictate searches.
   - If it finds matches, it displays matches in the window **E**.
   - If it doesn't find matches, it offers to create a new entry for you **F**. Follow the instructions in "To add a vocabulary entry" on page 70 to continue.

To add a vocabulary entry:

1. Follow the instructions in the section titled "To search for a vocabulary entry" on page 69 to make sure the entry you want to add doesn't already exist.

2. Do one of the following:

   ▸ If a similar word is found but it isn't exactly the word you need, click the + button at the bottom of the window.

   ▸ If the word is not found and Dictate offers to add the word for you **F**, click Yes. The word is added **G**; you're done.

3. Enter the word you want to add in the dialog that appears **H**.

4. Click OK. The word is added to the list.

To set vocabulary word options:

1. In the Vocabulary Editor window, select the word you want to set options for.

2. Click the *i* button at the bottom of the window.

   A pane slides up with additional options for the word **J**.

3. Set options as desired:

   ▸ **Written** is the written form of the word. You cannot change this.

   ▸ **Spoken** is an English equivalent to how the word is pronounced. You can set this option for User list words only; change it if the word is pronounced differently from the way it is spelled **K**.

TIP Clicking the Advanced disclosure triangle in the dialog that appears when adding a word **H** displays a field you can use to enter the spoken form of the word when the word is added.

G In this example, clicking the Yes button in **F** simply adds the word to the vocabulary list.

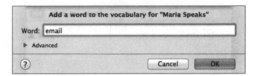

H Clicking the + button at the bottom of the Vocabulary Editor window displays a dialog you can use to enter the word you want to add.

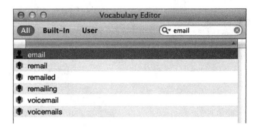

I In this example, I searched for *email*, the form preferred by my publisher. I didn't find it, so I added it. Since this is likely to conflict with the built-in entry, e-mail **E**, I'll need to delete that entry to use this one instead.

J Clicking the *i* button displays options for the selected entry.

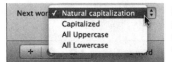

K You can enter the spoken pronunciation for a word.

L Choose a Next word capitalization option.

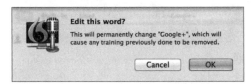

M Click OK in this dialog to save your changes.

▸ **Next word** lets you set capitalization for the word that follows this one when dictated. This option is primarily for use when adding punctuation to the vocabulary—for example, after a period, the next word is usually capitalized. Choose an option from the pop-up menu **L**. In most cases, you'll leave this set to Natural capitalization.

▸ **Insert Spaces** options let you specify how many spaces should be inserted before and after the word. Use the pop-up menus to make changes. You can set it to 0 or 1 before the word and 0, 1, or 2 after the word.

▸ **Lower case in titles** enables you to specify how the word should be typed when title case is enabled—for example, in the title of a book or chapter. For some short words, such as *in* and *or*, lowercase is preferred. You might also use this option if the word *always* begins with a lowercase letter, such as *iCloud*. Toggle the check box to set your preference for this word.

4. Press Return or click anywhere inside the window's list.

5. In the dialog that appears **M**, click OK.

   Your changes are saved.

TIP Clicking the Reset Defaults button resets all word options to their default settings. You can use this if you need to clear your changes and start over.

To train Dictate about the way you say a word:

1. In the Vocabulary Editor window, select the word you want to train Dictate for **J**.

2. Choose Train from the tools menu at the bottom of the window **N**.

3. An informational dialog appears **O**. Click Train.

   If the microphone is turned off, Dictate turns it on. It then displays a dialog while it waits for you to say the word.

4. Say the word three times.

   Each time you say it, Dictate fills in one third of a progress bar **P**. When you are finished, it displays a dialog telling you **Q**.

5. Click Close.

TIP Using this feature to train Dictate to understand the way you pronounce words—especially if your pronunciation isn't standard—can help improve its recognition capabilities.

TIP You can complete this process for any word in the Built-In or User vocabulary list.

N The tools menu at the bottom of the Vocabulary Editor window.

O This window explains what you'll need to do.

P In this example, I've said *Google Plus* once; I need to say it two more times to finish training.

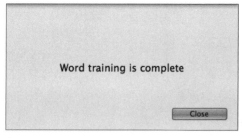

Q When training is complete, this dialog appears.

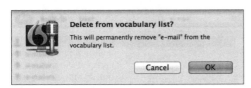

R Select the word you want to delete.

S Click OK in this dialog to delete the word.

To delete a vocabulary word:

1. Follow the instructions in the section titled "To search for a vocabulary entry" on page 69 to find the word you want to remove.

2. Select the word **R**.

3. Press the Delete key.

4. In the confirmation dialog that appears **S**, click OK.

   The word is removed from the vocabulary.

TIP Several sources, including the Dragon Dictate User Manual and the support articles on the Nuance website, state that Built-In vocabulary words cannot be deleted. As this book was written, however, it was possible to delete both Built-In and User vocabulary words using these instructions. Removing a word—for example, *e-mail*—is the only way to get Dictate to reliably use your preferred form of the same word—for example *email*.

CAUTION Do not delete vocabulary words you expect to use. Doing so could prevent Dictate from properly transcribing what you say.

Sharing Vocabulary Lists

In Dragon Dictate, a user's vocabulary list is stored within his or her profile file. In certain circumstances, it might be useful to quickly add those vocabulary words to another profile. For example:

- If you have more than one profile file because you use Dictate on more than one computer, you might find it useful to copy words from one profile to the other.

- If multiple users in your organization use Dictate to create documents with the same collection of technical words, you might find it useful to copy those words to each user's profile.

Fortunately, Dictate has you covered. It enables you to copy words from one profile to others. Just export words from one profile to an XML format file, move that file to another computer (if necessary), and import the file into another profile. Here's how it works.

To export vocabulary entries:

1. If necessary, open the Vocabulary Editor window (page 68).

2. Click the User button at the top of the window to display all user entries.

3. Click to select the entries you want to export 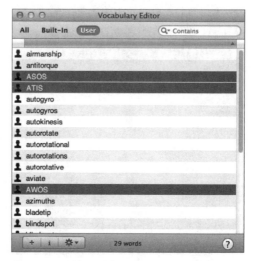.

TIP To select more than one entry, either click the first entry and then hold down Shift while clicking the last in a range or hold down Command while clicking each entry individually. Or, to select them all, choose Edit > Select All or press Command-A.

4. Choose Export from the tools menu at the bottom of the window 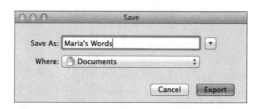.

Ⓐ In this example, I've selected three of the entries in my User vocabulary list.

Ⓑ You can find the Import and Export commands on the tools menu at the bottom of the Vocabulary Editor window.

Ⓒ Use a standard Save dialog to save the vocabulary list. (The appearance of this dialog may differ, depending on whether it is expanded to show additional file location options.)

D Click OK in this dialog when the export is complete.

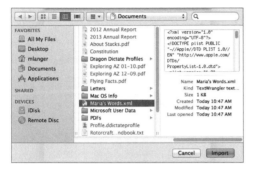

E Use a standard Open dialog to locate and select the file containing the exported vocabulary words.

F Click OK in this dialog when the import is complete.

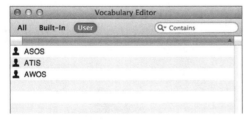

G The words that were in the file are imported into the User vocabulary list.

5. In the Save dialog that appears **C**, enter a name and choose a location for the exported list.

6. Click Export.

   Dictate creates and saves an XML file containing the User list of vocabulary words.

7. In the Export Complete dialog **D**, click OK.

To import a user vocabulary list:

1. If necessary, open the Vocabulary Editor window (page 68).

2. Choose Import from the tools menu at the bottom of the window **B**.

3. In the Open dialog that appears **E**, locate and select the exported vocabulary file that you want to import.

4. Click Import.

   The words in the file are imported into the profile.

5. Click OK in the Import Complete dialog that appears **F**.

   The words you imported appear in the User vocabulary list **G**.

6

Controlling Your Computer

The previous chapters have concentrated on one very common use for Dragon Dictate: transcribing and editing the text you dictate. But Dictate can do much more than that. It can enable you to control many computer operations without touching your keyboard or mouse.

One of the ways Dictate does this is through the use of *global commands* that can be understood and interpreted in Command mode no matter which application or window is active. These commands can be broken down into three groups:

- **Global Commands** are voice commands that perform a specific task.

- **Key Commands** are voice commands that make keystrokes.

- **Mouse Commands** are voice commands that control mouse movement and activity.

This chapter covers many of Dictate's global commands and explains how you can use them for hands-free computer control. But first, it'll take a closer look at the Available Commands window, which lists the commands you can use.

In This Chapter

The Available Commands Window

The Available Commands window 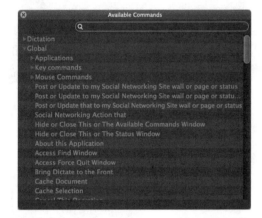 lists all of the commands currently available for use with Dictate. It's an extremely useful tool for quickly learning the command you need to get a task done.

Because the Available Commands window only lists those commands *currently* available, its content changes each time you change modes, switch windows, switch applications, or do something else to change the state of your computer. In addition, because only a handful of commands are available in Sleep mode **B**, it's best consulted either with the microphone off or awake, in Dictation mode **A** or Command mode.

The Available Commands window organizes commands by group, making it a bit easier to find the command you're looking for. It also has its own Spotlight search box, which you can use to find commands based on a search word or phrase.

To view the Available Commands window:

Do one of the following:

- Say *Show Available Commands*.
- Choose Window > Show Available Commands.

A The Available Commands window, in Dictation mode with the Dictate application active.

B In Sleep mode, the Available Commands window isn't a very useful reference tool—unless all you need to know is how to wake Dictate.

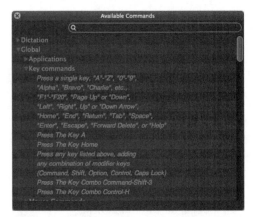

In this example, I've displayed the commands under the Key Commands heading.

You can enter a search word or phrase to display related commands

To show or hide groups of commands:

Click the disclosure triangle beside a command heading.

- When the triangle points down, a list of commands beneath that heading appears Ⓐ Ⓑ Ⓒ.

- When the triangle points right, the heading's commands are hidden Ⓐ Ⓒ.

To search for a command:

1. In the Available Commands, window, click in the Spotlight search box.

2. Dictate or type a search word or phrase.

3. The results appear immediately Ⓓ. If necessary, click disclosure triangles to display hidden commands.

TIP To clear the search results, click the X button on the right end of the Spotlight search box Ⓓ.

To hide the Available Commands window:

Do one of the following:

- Say **Hide Available Commands**.

- Choose Window > Hide Available Commands.

- Click the Available Commands window's close button.

Global Commands

Global commands are voice commands that perform a specific task no matter which application or window is active.

Earlier chapters of this book already covered some global commands—for example *Microphone Off*, *Numbers Mode*, and *Scratch Word*. Although these commands perform tasks specific to Dragon Dictate, they work in any application or mode.

But there are many other commands that perform tasks that are unrelated to Dictate's operations or feature set. I've broken them down into several groups based on where they work and what they do:

- **Mac OS Commands** (Table 6.1) activate features that are part of the Macintosh operating system or work throughout Mac OS. This includes commands for restarting the computer, capturing a screen, and hiding or displaying active applications.

- **Application Commands** (Table 6.2) activate features within applications. This includes commands for creating and opening documents, copying and pasting text, and quitting.

TIP Application-specific commands—those commands that only work with specific applications—are covered in Chapter 7.

- **Dialog Commands** (Table 6.3) activate buttons and fields in dialog boxes. This includes clicking button and switching fields.

TIP Mouse commands, which are also handy in dialogs, are covered in the section titled "Mouse Commands" on page 87.

- **Search Commands** (Table 6.4) enable you to search for items or information on your computer or the Internet. You can use these commands to search the Finder, Mail, or the Internet.

- **Information Commands** (Table 6.5) let you use special Dictate commands to get information from your computer, including the current date and time and definitions for words.

Most of the commands in this part of the chapter are self-explanatory. Using a few of the less obvious commands is covered in detail on the following pages. Experiment with them to see how they work for you.

TIP Dictate supports many commands—perhaps more than you can remember! Don't panic when you browse these lists. Concentrate on remembering the commands you use most; no need to remember the commands you'll never use.

TABLE 6.1 Global Commands for Working with Mac OS

To Do This:	Say This:
Open a Finder Search window	*Access Find Window*
Open the Force Quit window	*Access Force Quit Window*
Create a screen shot of the entire screen	*Capture Screen*
Create a screen shot of a selected part of the screen	*Capture Selection*
Turn on Dock hiding	*Turn Dock Hiding On*
Turn off Dock hiding	*Turn Dock Hiding Off*
Display all windows with Exposé *	*Exposé All Windows*
Display the active application's windows with Exposé *	*Exposé Application Windows*
Display the Desktop with Exposé	*Exposé Desktop*
Switch to Space 1 *	*Switch to Space One*
Switch to Space 2 *	*Switch to Space Two*
Switch to Space 3 *	*Switch to Space Three*
Switch to Space 4 *	*Switch to Space Four*
Open or activate a specific application	*Activate* application name
Quit a specific application	*Quit* application name
Activate Dragon Dictate	*Bring Dragon Dictate to the Front*
Switch to the next open application	*Switch to Next Application*
Switch to the previous application	*Switch to Previous Application*
Hide the current application	*Hide This Application*
Hide all applications other than the active application	*Hide All Applications* or *Hide The Other Applications*
Show all open applications	*Show All Applications*
Cancel the current operation	*Cancel This Operation*
Put the computer to sleep	*Put Computer to Sleep*
Force the computer to go to sleep	*Special Sleep*
Restart the computer	*Restart the Computer*
Restart the computer without waiting for tasks to finish	*Special Restart*

* This command is not available in Mac OS X Lion.

To use a global command

Say the command (refer to Tables 6.1 to 6.5).

If Dictate understood the command, it performs it. Otherwise, it either does nothing or makes an alert sound.

TIP Although many Global commands should work in both Dictation and Command mode, they work most reliably in Command mode. If, in Dictation mode, Dictate types your command instead of performing it, say Undo Dictation, switch to Command mode, and try again.

TIP In some instances, if a command is not available, an error message may appear **A**. Click OK (or say *Press OK*) to dismiss it and continue working.

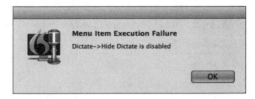

A If Dictate is the active application and you issue a command that is not available, a dialog like this may appear.

TABLE 6.2 Global Commands for Working with the Active Application

To Do This:	Say This:
Open the About window	*About This Application*
Quit the application	*Quit This Application*
Choose File > New	*File New*
Choose File > Open	*File Open*
Choose File > Close	*File Close*
Choose File > Save	*Save This Document*
Choose Edit > Undo	*Undo Last Action*
Choose Edit > Redo	*Redo Last Action*
Choose Edit > Copy	*Copy Selection*
Choose Edit > Paste	*Paste from Clipboard*
Choose Edit > Select All	*Select All*
Switch to the next window	*Next Application Window*
Switch to the previous window	*Previous Application Window*

TABLE 6.3 Global Commands for Working with Dialog Boxes

To Do This:	Say This:
Select the next field	*Next Field*
Select the previous field	*Previous Field*
Click the Cancel button	*Press Cancel*
Click the Continue button	*Press Continue*
Click the Don't Save button	*Press Don't Save*
Click the OK button	*Press OK*
Click the Save button	*Press Save*

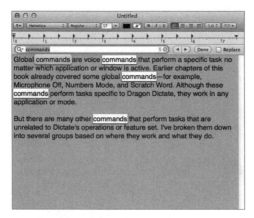

B In this example, I searched a TextEdit document by saying **Search This Document for Commands**. TextEdit's search feature highlights the matches.

C Saying **Search Finder For John** on my computer performs a Spotlight search with these results.

To search a document for text:

1. If necessary, activate the document window.

2. Say **Search This Document For searchtext**.

   So, for example, if you wanted to search a document for the word *commands*, you'd say **Search This Document For Commands**.

   The application's search feature activates and it begins a search for the word or phrase you specified **B**.

To search the Finder for text:

Say **Search Finder For searchtext**. So, for example, if you wanted to search the Finder for a file containing the name *John*, you'd say **Search Finder for John**.

The Spotlight menu is activated and the search word is entered into the search field. A list of matches appears automatically **C**.

TABLE 6.4 Global Commands for Searching

To Do This:	Say This:
Activate the application's search feature	*Search This Document*
Search the current document for specific text	*Search This Document For* searchtext
Repeat the last search	*Search Again*
Search the Finder for specific text	*Search Finder For* searchtext
Search Mail for specific text	*Search Mail For* searchtext
Search the Internet for specific text	*Search* searchprovider *for* searchtext

To search the Mail app for text:

Say **Search Mail For** searchtext.

So, for example, if you wanted to search Mac OS's Mail application for a messages from or containing the name *John*, you'd say **Search Mail for John**.

A few things happen **D**:

- If Mail isn't already open, it launches.
- The search word or phrase you specified is entered in Mail's Spotlight search box.
- A list of matches appears in a menu beneath the Spotlight search box.
- Messages that match the search word or phrase appear in the message list.

To search the Internet for text:

Say **Search** searchprovider **For** searchtext.

So, for example, if you wanted to search Google for *Dragon Dictate*, you'd say **Search Google For Dragon Dictate**. Or if you wanted to search Bing for *Peachpit Press*, you'd say **Search Bing For Peachpit Press**.

A few things happen **E** **F**:

- If Safari (or your default web browser) isn't already open, it launches.
- A URL containing a fully formed search string for the search provider you specified is entered into the address bar.
- The results of the search appear in the web browser window.

D Saying **Search Mail For John** on my computer opens Mail, performs a search, and displays matches.

E In this example, I said **Search Google for Dragon Dictate** ...

F ... and in this example, I said **Search Bing for Peachpit Press**.

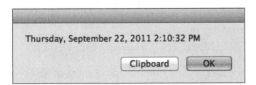

Thursday, September 22, 2011 2:10:32 PM

Clipboard | OK

G Say *Show The Date And Time* to display a dialog like this—with the current time, of course!

H In this example, I said *Show Definition For Helicopter*.

To display the date and time:

1. Say *Show The Date And Time*.

   A window containing the current date and time appears **G**.

2. To dismiss the window, say *Press OK*.

TIP In step 1, you can click the Clipboard button to copy the date and time to the Clipboard. You can then paste it into a document.

To display the definition for a word:

Say *Show Definition For* word.

So, to get the definition for the word helicopter, you'd say *Show Definition For Helicopter*.

A few things happen **H**:

- If the Dictionary app isn't already opened, it launches.

- The word you specified is entered into the search box.

- The word's entry appears in the window.

TABLE 6.5 Global Commands for Getting Information

To Do This:	Say This:
Display a window containing the current date and time	*Show The Date And Time*
Display the Dictionary definition for a specific word	*Show Definition For* word

Key Commands

Key commands enable you to use verbal commands in Command mode to enter keystrokes with Dragon Dictate. This makes it possible to use shortcut keys to send commands to Mac OS or the active application.

When you say a key command, Dictate attempts to apply it to the active application or to Mac OS as appropriate. For example, if you used the key command for Command-W, the active application's topmost window would likely close—because Command-W is probably the shortcut key to close a window in that application. But if you used the key command for Command-Shift-3, the command would be interpreted by Mac OS, which uses that keystroke to capture a screen shot.

If the key command you said was valid—in other words, it can be understood by Dictate—but that keystroke doesn't do any-thing in the active application or Mac OS, nothing happens.

There are two kinds of key commands:

- **Single key** commands consist of just one key. Examples include:
    - ▸ *Press The Key Home*
    - ▸ *Press The Key Escape*
- **Key combinations** consist of one or more modifier keys with another key. Some examples are:
    - ▸ *Press The Key Combo Command N*
    - ▸ *Press the Key Combo Command Shift Sierra*
    - ▸ *Press The Key Combo Option Command One*
    - ▸ *Press The Key Combo Command-Tab*

It's impossible to list all of the key commands here. Instead, you can consult Table 6.6 for instructions on how to build your own valid key commands.

TABLE 6.6 Commands for Typing Keystrokes

Start by saying this:	add this:	If the keystroke is a key combination, add one or more of these modifiers:	And then say one of these key names:
Press The Key	*Combo*	*Command* *Shift* *Option* *Control* *Caps Lock*	Letter names (*A* through *Z*) International Radio Alphabet Letter Names (*Alpha* through *Zulu*) See Table 3.6 on page 34. Digit Names (*Zero* through *Nine*) F-Key Names (*F One* through *F Twenty*) Named Keys:

Left Arrow	*Home*	*Return*
Right Arrow	*End*	*Enter*
Up Arrow	*Page Up*	*Space*
Down Arrow	*Page Down*	*Tab*
Escape	*Forward Delete*	*Help*

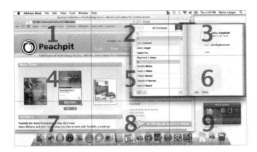

A Here's a typical screen with the regular mouse grid displayed ...

B ... and here's a zoomed-in view of the same screen with the small mouse grid displayed.

TABLE 6.7 Mouse Grid Commands

To Do This:	Say This:
Display the mouse grid	*MouseGrid* or *Open MouseGrid*
Display the Small mouse grid	*Small MouseGrid* or *Open Small MouseGrid*
Remove the mouse grid	*Cancel*

Mouse Commands

Mouse commands enable you to manipulate your computer with Dragon Dictate by verbally directing mouse movements and clicks. You do this in Command mode with three kinds of commands:

- **Mouse Grid** commands (Table 6.7) place a grid with numbered squares onscreen. You say the number of the square to zoom into that area with another, smaller grid. Repeat that process to pinpoint an exact location onscreen. There are two mouse grids: the regular mouse grid fills the entire screen **A** and the small mouse grid is smaller and appears around the mouse pointer **B**.

- **Move Mouse** commands (Tables 6.8 and 6.9) enable you to move your mouse pointer up, down, left, or right. You can set the mouse movement speed or include a measurement you specify in points, inches, or centimeters.

- **Mouse Click** commands (Table 6.10) enable you to click, double-click, triple-click, or hold and release the mouse. You can even include modifier keys such as Command, Shift, Option, Control, or Caps Lock.

This part of the chapter explores how you can use Dictate to control your computer with your mouse pointer.

To use the mouse grid:

1. If necessary, switch to Command mode.

2. Say one of the following:

   ▸ To display the regular mouse grid, say *MouseGrid*.

   ▸ To display the small mouse grid around the pointer, say *Small MouseGrid*.

   The mouse grid appears .

3. Say the number for the grid square you want to work with.

   The mouse grid is redrawn in that grid square .

4. Repeat step 3 as necessary to close in on the area you want to work with .

   Eventually, the grid will become too small to display the numbers and a magnification window will appear onscreen.

5. When the mouse pointer is on the location you want, use a mouse click command (Table 6.9) to perform the click action you want.

6. To remove the mouse grid, say *Cancel*.

TIP Each time you say the number of a grid square, the mouse pointer moves to the middle of square 5.

Starting with the mouse grid in A, I said *Six*, *Eight*, *Four*, and *Three* to close in on the Edit button in the Address Book window.

TABLE 6.8 Move Mouse Commands

To Do This:	Say This:
Move the mouse up	*Move Mouse Up*
Move the mouse down	*Move Mouse Down*
Move the mouse left	*Move Mouse Left*
Move the mouse right	*Move Mouse Right*
Move the mouse diagonally	*Move Mouse Left And Up* or *Move Mouse Right And Up* or *Move Mouse Left And Down* or *Move Mouse Right And Down*
Move the mouse faster	*Faster*
Move the mouse slower	*Slower*
Stop moving the mouse	*Stop*
Move the mouse a certain direction by a specific amount	*Move The Mouse direction units unitname* (Refer to Table 6.9.)

To move the mouse pointer:

1. Say one of the commands in the first five rows of Table 6.8.

   The mouse pointer begins to move in the direction you specified.

2. To change the speed of movement, say one of the following:

   ▸ To move the mouse pointer faster, say *Faster*.

   ▸ To move the mouse pointer slower, say *Slower*.

3. Repeat steps 1 and 2 as necessary to get the pointer in the desired position.

4. Say *Stop*.

To move the mouse pointer a certain direction by a certain amount:

Say a valid command using components shown in Table 6.9.

The mouse pointer moves the direction and amount you specified.

TABLE 6.9 Commands for Moving the Mouse Pointer a Specific Direction by a Specific Amount

Say this:	Then say a direction:	Add the number of units:	And then add the unit name:
Move The Mouse	*Up*	any number from 1 to 100	*Points*
	Down		*Inches*
	Left		*Centimeters*
	Right		
	Left And Up		
	Right And Up		
	Left And Down		
	Right And Down		

To click the mouse:

1. Position the mouse where you want to click.

2. Say one of the mouse click commands in Table 6.10. If you want to click with a modifier key held down, be sure to say the name of the modifier key (Command, Shift, Option, Control, or Caps Lock) before the mouse click command.

   The mouse clicks.

To click & hold the mouse:

1. Position the mouse where you want to click and hold.

2. Say *Hold Mouse*.

   A purple circle pulsates around the mouse pointer to indicate that it is being held **G**.

To release the mouse:

Say *Release Mouse*.

The mouse pointer is released, the blue circle disappears, and the mouse pointer functions normally.

G In this example, I used the mouse grid to position the pointer and then said *Hold Mouse*.

TABLE 6.10 Mouse Click Commands

To Do This:	Say This:
Click	*Mouse Click*
Double-click	*Mouse Double Click*
Triple-click	*Mouse Triple Click*
Hold down a modifier key while clicking, double-clicking, or triple-clicking	*modifierkey Mouse Click* or *modifierkey Mouse Double Click* or *modifierkey Mouse Triple Click*
Click and hold the mouse pointer	*Hold Mouse*
Release the mouse	*Release Mouse*

Using Application Commands

As discussed in Chapter 6, Dragon Dictate's global commands work in all applications. But Dictate also supports a huge collection of application-specific commands. These commands make it possible to perform tasks in a number of Mac OS applications, including Dragon Dictate, Finder, TextEdit, Microsoft Word, Safari, Mail, and iCal. And Dictate's sharing feature also makes it possible to update your Twitter and Facebook accounts using verbal commands.

Commands for a specific application work only when that application is active. You can use a global command, **Activate application name**, to make an application active, if necessary, before saying a command.

This chapter tells you about the application commands that are built into Dictate. It also provides lists of the commands you can use while working with each of these applications.

Command Overview

Dragon Dictate's application commands have many things in common. For example, many of the same commands are repeated from one application to another. This helps make some of the most basic commands— such as **Close This Window** or **Copy The Selection**—easier to remember.

Another thing to keep in mind as you learn these commands is that some command words are used interchangeably. (You can see a list of these word pairs in Table 7.1.) This means that a command can be constructed with either of the words in the pair.

You can see a list of commands for the active application at any time by displaying the Available Commands window (page 78) and clicking the disclosure triangle beside the name of the active application to see the list of commands 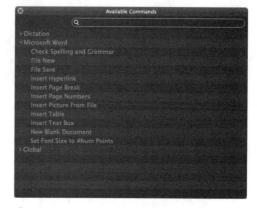.

Don't let the lists of commands on the following pages intimidate you. You don't need to learn them all. Instead, learn them as you work by consulting these lists when you need a command. You'll find that the ones you use most are quickly committed to memory.

TIP To save space in the tables of commands throughout this chapter, I've shown word pairs (Table 7.1) with a slash between them. Say either word in the pair when speaking the command. For example *Close This/The Window* means you can say *Close This Window* or *Close The Window*.

TIP Some commands include a variable—normally specific dictated text or the name of an item. In the tables throughout this chapter, variables in commands are presented in plain (not italic) text. For example *Search This Document For* searchtext means to say the italicized words followed by the text you are searching for.

A In this example, Microsoft Word is the active application. I can see Word commands in the Available Commands window.

TABLE 7.1 Common Command Word Pairs

Say This:	Or This:
This	*The*
Access	*Show*
Close	*Hide*
Make	*Create*

Dragon Dictate Commands

Dragon Dictate commands work when the Dictate application is active. These commands, which are listed in table 7.2, enable you to access just about every Dictate menu command.

TABLE 7.2 Dragon Dictate Commands

To do this:	Say this:
Choose Dictate > About Dictate	*About This/The Application*
Choose Dictate > Check for Updates	*Access/Show Check For Updates Window*
Choose Dictate > Preferences	*Access/Show Preferences Window*
Choose Dictate > Hide Dictate	*Hide This/The Application*
Choose Dictate > Hide Others	*Hide Other Applications*
Choose Dictate > Show All	*Show All Applications* or *Show Other Applications*
Choose File > New Note Pad	*Make/Create New Note Pad*
Choose File > New Command	*Make/Create New Command*
Choose File > Open	*Access/Show Open Window*
Choose File > Open Recent > Clear Menu	*Clear Recent Menu*
Choose File > Close	*Close This/The Window*
Choose File > Close All (You must hold down the Option key to see this command.)	*Close All*
Choose File > Save	*Save This/The Document*
Choose File > Save As	*Access/Show Save As Window*
Choose File > Revert to Saved	*Revert To Last Saved Version*
Choose File > Print	*Access/Show Print Window*
Choose File > Command Export	*Access/Show Command Export Window*
Choose Edit > Undo	*Undo Last Action*
Choose Edit > Redo	*Redo Last Action*
Choose Edit > Cut	*Cut This/The Selection*
Choose Edit > Copy	*Copy This/The Selection*
Choose Edit > Paste	*Paste From Clipboard*
Choose Edit > Paste and Match Style	*Paste And Match Style*

table continues on next page

TABLE 7.2 *continued*

To do this:	Say this:
Choose Edit > Delete	***Delete This/The Selection***
Choose Edit > Select All	***Select All***
Choose Edit > Find > Find	***Access/Show This/The Find Window*** or ***Search This/The Document***
Choose Edit > Find > Find Next	***Find Next***
Open the Find window and begin a search for specific text	***Search This/The Document For*** searchtext
Repeat the previous search	***Search Again***
Choose Edit > Find > Find Previous	***Find Previous***
Choose Edit > Find > Use Selection for Find	***Use Selection For Find***
Choose Edit > Find > Jump to Selection	***Jump To Selection***
Choose Edit > Spelling > Show Spelling and Grammar *or* Choose Edit > Spelling > Hide Spelling and Grammar	***Toggle This/The Spelling And Grammar Window***
Choose Edit > Spelling > Check Spelling	***Check Spelling***
Choose Edit > Special Characters	***Access/Show Special Characters Window***
Choose Tools > Profiles	***Access/Show This/The Profiles Window***
Choose Tools > Commands	***Access/Show Commands Window***
Choose Tools > Vocabulary Editor	***Access/Show Vocabulary Editor Window***
Choose Tools > Microphone Setup	***Access/Show This/The Microphone Setup Window***
Choose Tools > Voice Training	***Access/Show Voice Training Window***
Choose Tools > Vocabulary Training	***Access/Show Vocabulary Training Window***
Choose Tools > Vocabulary Training from Selection	***Access/Show Vocabulary Training From Selection Window***
Choose Format > Text > Align Left	***Align This/The Text Left***
Choose Format > Text > Center	***Align This/The Text Center***
Choose Format > Text > Justify	***Justify This/The Selection***
Choose Format > Text > Align Right	***Align This/The Text Right***

table continues on next page

TABLE 7.2 *continued*

To do this:	Say this:
Choose Window > Minimize	*Minimize This/The Window*
Choose Window > Minimize All (You must hold down the Option key to see this command.)	*Minimize All Windows*
Choose Window > Zoom	*Zoom This/The Window*
Choose Window > Bring All to Front	*Bring All Windows To The Front*
Choose Window > Arrange in Front (You must hold down the Option key to see this command.)	*Arrange In Front*
Choose Help > Dictate Help	*Access/Show Dictate Help*
Choose Help > Tips & Tricks	*Access/Show Tips And Tricks*
Choose Help > Release Notes	*Access/Show Release Notes*
Choose Help > Quickstart Guide	*Access/Show Quickstart Guide*
Choose Help > User Manual	*Access/Show User Manual*
Choose Help > Send Email to Tech Support	*Send Email To Tech Support*

Finder Commands

Finder commands (Table 7.3) work with the Mac OS X Finder. Dictate includes voice commands for most Finder menu commands.

TIP You may also find Mouse commands (page 87) useful when verbally manipulating items in the Finder.

TABLE 7.3 Finder Commands

To do this:	Say this:
Choose Finder > About Finder	*About This/The Finder*
Choose Finder > Preferences	*Access/Show Preferences Window*
Choose Finder > Empty Trash	*Empty Trash*
Choose Finder > Secure Empty Trash	*Secure Empty Trash*
Choose Finder > Hide Finder	*Hide/Close This Application*
Choose Finder > Hide Others	*Hide/Close Other Applications*
Choose Finder > Show All	*Access/Show All Applications*
Choose File > New Finder Window	*New Finder Window*
Choose File > New Folder	*Make/Create New Folder*
Choose File > New Smart Folder	*Make/Create New Smart Folder*
Choose File > New Burn Folder	*Make/Create New Burn Folder*
Choose File > Open	*Open Selection*
Choose File > Print	*Print This/The Document*
Choose File > Close Window	*Close This/The Window*
Choose File > Close All Windows (You must hold down the Option key to see this command.)	*Close All Windows*
Choose File > Get Info	*Get Info*
Choose File > Show Inspector (You must hold down the Option key to see this command.)	*Show/Access Inspector*
Choose File > Hide Inspector (You must hold down the Option key to see this command.)	*Hide/Close Inspector*
Choose File > Compress	*Compress This/The Selection*
Choose File > Duplicate	*Duplicate This/The Selection*
Choose File > Make Alias	*Make/Create Alias*
Choose File > Quick Look	*Quick Look Selection*

table continues on next page

TABLE 7.3 *continued*

To do this:	Say this:
Choose File > Slideshow (You must hold down the Option key to see this command.)	*Slideshow Selection*
Choose File > Show Original	*Access/Show Original*
Choose File > Add to Sidebar	*Add To Sidebar*
Choose File > Move to Trash	*Move To Trash*
Choose File > Eject	*Eject Selection*
Choose File > Burn to Disc	*Access/Show Burn Disc Window*
Choose File > Find	*Access/Show Find Window*
Choose Edit > Undo	*Undo Last Action*
Choose Edit > Cut	*Cut This/The Selection*
Choose Edit > Copy	*Copy This/The Selection*
Choose Edit > Paste	*Paste From Clipboard*
Choose Edit > Select All	*Select All*
Choose Edit > Deselect All (You must hold down the Option key to see this command.)	*Deselect All*
Choose Edit > Show Clipboard	*Access/Show Clipboard*
Choose Edit > Special Characters	*Display Special Characters Window*
Choose View > As Icons	*View As Icons*
Choose View > As List	*View As List*
Choose View > As Columns	*View As Columns*
Choose View > As Cover Flow	*View As Cover Flow*
Choose View > Clean Up	*Clean Up This/The Folder/Window*
Choose View > Clean Up Selection	*Clean Up Selection*
Choose View > Arrange By Name	*Arrange By Name*
Choose View > Arrange By Kind	*Arrange By Kind*
Choose View > Arrange By Date Modified	*Arrange By Date Modified*
Choose View > Arrange By Date Created	*Arrange By Date Created*
Choose View > Arrange By Size	*Arrange By Size*
Choose View > Arrange By Label	*Arrange By Label*
Choose View > Show Path Bar	*Access/Show Path Bar*
Choose View > Hide Path Bar	*Hide Path Bar*
Choose View > Show Status Bar	*Access/Show Status Bar*
Choose View > Hide Status Bar	*Hide Status Bar*
Choose View > Show Toolbar	*Access/Show Toolbar*

table continues on next page

TABLE 7.3 *continued*

To do this:	Say this:
Choose View > Hide Toolbar	*Hide Toolbar*
Choose View > Customize Toolbar	*Access/Show Customize Toolbar Folder/Window*
Choose View > Show View Options	*Access/Show View Options*
Choose View > Hide View Options	*Hide View Options*
Choose Go > Back	*Go Back/Previous*
Choose Go > Forward	*Go Forward/Next*
Choose Go > Enclosing Folder	*Go To Enclosing Folder*
Choose Go > Documents	*Go To The Documents Folder/Window*
Choose Go > Desktop	*Go To The Desktop*
Choose Go > Downloads	*Go To The Downloads Folder/Window*
Choose Go > Home	*Go To The Home Folder/Window*
Choose Go > Computer	*Go To The Computer Folder/Window*
Choose Go > Network	*Go To The Network Folder/Window*
Choose Go > iDisk > My iDisk	*Go To My iDisk*
Choose Go > iDisk > Other User's Public Folder	*Access/Show Other User's Public Folder*
Choose Go > Applications	*Go To The Applications Folder*
Choose Go > Utilities	*Go To The Utilities Folder/Window*
Choose Go > Recent Folders > Clear Menu	*Clear Recent Folders Menu*
Choose Go > Go to Folder	*Access/Show Go To Folder Window*
Choose Go > Connect to Server	*Access/Show Connect To Server Window*
Choose Window > Minimize	*Minimize This/The Window*
Choose Window > Minimize All (You must hold down the Option key to see this command.)	*Minimize All Windows*
Choose Window > Zoom	*Zoom This/The Window*
Choose Window > Cycle Through Windows	*Cycle Through Windows*
Choose Window > Bring All to Front	*Bring All To Front*
Choose Help > Mac Help (Snow Leopard only)	*Access/Show/Display Mac Help*
Choose Show Package Contents from a window's Action menu	*Access/Show Package Contents Of Selection*
Click the Cancel button	*Press Cancel Button*
Click the Connect button	*Press Connect Button*
Click the Done button	*Press Done Button*
Select the name of the selected icon	*Select Name Of Selection*
Select the next item alphabetically	*Select Next Name*
Select the previous item alphabetically	*Select Previous Name*

TextEdit Commands

Dragon Dictate supports many of TextEdit's menu commands (Table 7.4) when TextEdit is the active application.

TABLE 7.4 TextEdit Commands

To do this:	Say this:
Choose TextEdit > About TextEdit	*About This Application*
Choose TextEdit > Preferences	*Access/Show Preferences Window*
Choose TextEdit > Hide TextEdit	*Hide This Application*
Choose TextEdit > Hide Others	*Hide Other Applications*
Choose TextEdit > Show All	*Show All Applications*
Choose TextEdit > Quit TextEdit	*Quit This/The Application*
Choose File > New	*Make/Create A New Document*
Choose File > Open	*Open A Document*
Choose File > Open Recent > Clear Menu	*Clear Recent Menu*
Choose File > Close	*Close This/The Window*
Choose File > Close All (You must hold down the Option key to see this command.)	*Close All Windows*
Choose File > Save	*Save This/The Document*
Choose File > Save As	*Access/Show Save As Window*
Choose File > Revert to Saved	*Revert To Last Saved Version*
Choose File > Show Properties	*Show Properties Window*
Choose File > Hide Properties	*Hide Properties Window*
Choose File > Page Setup	*Access/Show Page Setup Window*
Choose File > Print	*Print This/The Document*
Choose Edit > Undo	*Undo Last Action*
Choose Edit > Redo	*Redo Last Action*
Choose Edit > Cut	*Cut This/The Selection*
Choose Edit > Copy	*Copy This/The Selection*
Choose Edit > Paste	*Paste From Clipboard*
Choose Edit > Paste and Match Style	*Paste And Match Style*
Choose Edit > Delete	*Delete This/The Selection*
Choose Edit > Complete	*Complete This/The Selection*
Choose Edit > Select All	*Select All*

table continues on next page

TABLE 7.4 *continued*

To do this:	Say this:
Choose Edit > Insert > Line Break	*Insert Line Break*
Choose Edit > Insert > Paragraph Break	*Insert Paragraph Break*
Choose Edit > Insert > Page Break	*Insert Page Break*
Choose Edit > Edit Link	*Show Link Window*
Choose Edit > Find > Find	*Access/Show Find Window*
Choose Edit > Find > Find Next	*Find Next*
Choose Edit > Find > Find Previous	*Find Previous*
Choose Edit > Find > Use Selection for Find	*Use Selection For Find*
Choose Edit > Find > Jump to Selection	*Jump To Selection*
Choose Edit > Find > Select Line	*Access/Show Select Line Window*
Choose Edit > Spelling > Show Spelling and Grammar	*Show/Display Spelling And Grammar Window*
Choose Edit > Spelling > Hide Spelling and Grammar	*Hide Spelling and Grammar Window*
Choose Edit > Spelling > Check Document Now	*Check Spelling And Grammar Of This/The Document*
Choose Edit > Spelling > Check Spelling While Typing	*Turn Check Spelling While Typing Off* or *Turn Check Spelling While Typing On*
Choose Edit > Spelling > Check Grammar With Spelling	*Turn Check Grammar With Spelling Off* or *Turn Check Grammar With Spelling On*
Choose Edit > Substitutions > Smart Copy/Paste	*Turn Substitutions Smart Copy And Paste Off* or *Turn Smart Copy And Paste On*
Choose Edit > Substitutions > Smart Quotes	*Turn Smart Quotes Off* or *Turn Smart Quotes On*
Choose Edit > Substitutions > Smart Links	*Turn Smart Links Off* or *Turn Smart Links On*
Choose Edit > Special Characters	*Display Special Characters Window*
Choose Format > Font > Show Fonts	*Show/Display Fonts Palette*
Choose Format > Font > Hide Fonts	*Hide This/The Fonts Palette*
Choose Format > Font > Bold	*Make This/The Selection Bold*
Choose Format > Font > Italic	*Make This/The Selection Italic*
Choose Format > Font > Outline	*Make This/The Selection Outline*
Choose Format > Font > Underline	*Make This/The Selection Underlined*
Choose Format > Font > Bigger	*Make This/The Selection Bigger*
Choose Format > Font > Smaller	*Make This/The Selection Smaller*

table continues on next page

TABLE 7.4 *continued*

To do this:	Say this:
Choose Format > Font > Show Colors	*Show Colors Palette*
Choose Format > Font > Hide Colors	*Hide Colors Palette*
Choose Format > Text > Align Left	*Align This/The Text Left*
Choose Format > Text > Center	*Align This/The Text Center*
Choose Format > Text > Justify	*Justify This/The Selection*
Choose Format > Text > Align Right	*Align This/The Text Right*
Choose Format > Text > Writing Direction > (Paragraph) Right to Left	*Change Text Writing Direction*
Choose Format > Text > Show Ruler	*Show/Display The Text Ruler*
Choose Format > Text > Hide Ruler	*Hide Text Ruler*
Choose Format > Text > Copy Ruler	*Copy Text Ruler*
Choose Format > Text > Paste Ruler	*Paste Text Ruler*
Choose Format > Text > Spacing	*Access/Show Text Spacing Window*
Choose Format > Make Plain Text	*Make This/The Selection Plain Text* or *Convert Document To Plain Text*
Choose Format > Make Rich Text	*Convert Document To Rich Text*
Choose Format > Prevent Editing	*Turn Prevent Editing On*
Choose Format > Allow Editing	*Turn Prevent Editing Off*
Choose Format > Wrap to Page	*Wrap Text To Page*
Choose Format Allow Hyphenation	*Turn Hyphenation On*
Choose Format Do Not Allow Hyphenation	*Turn Hyphenation Off*
Choose Format > List	*Access/Show List Window*
Choose Format > Table	*Access/Show Table Window*
Choose Window > Minimize	*Minimize This/The Window*
Choose Window > Minimize All (You must hold down the Option key to see this command.)	*Minimize All Windows*
Choose Window > Zoom	*Zoom This/The Window*
Choose Window > Bring All to Front	*Bring All Windows To Front*
Choose Help > TextEdit Help	*Display Help*

Microsoft Word Commands

Although Dragon Dictate fully supports Microsoft Word for text dictation, it currently works with just a handful of application commands. The commands listed in Table 7.5 refer to menu commands found in Word 2011; they should work for equivalent menu commands in Word 2008.

TABLE 7.5 Microsoft Word Commands

To do this:	Say this:
Choose Word > Quit Word	*Quit Microsoft Word*
Choose File > New Blank Document	*File New* or *File New Blank Document*
Choose File > Close	*File Close*
Choose File > Save	*File Save*
Choose Insert > Break > Page Break	*Insert Page Break*
Choose Insert > Page Numbers	*Insert Page Numbers*
Choose Insert > Table	*insert Table*
Choose Insert > Photo > Picture from File	*Insert Picture From File*
Choose Insert > Text Box	*Insert Text Box*
Choose Insert > Hyperlink	*Insert Hyperlink*
Set the font size of selected text to *n* points	*Set Font Size To n Points*
Choose Tools > Spelling and Grammar	*Check Spelling And Grammar*

Safari Commands

Dictate includes extensive support for Apple's Safari web browser, from triggering menu commands to jumping to specific bookmarks. Table 7.6 lists the built-in commands you can use when Safari is the active application. These commands were tested with Safari 5.1 running on Mac OS X Lion.

TABLE 7.6 Safari Commands

To do this:	Say this:
Choose Safari > About Safari	*About This/The Application*
Choose Safari > Report Bugs to Apple	*Access/Show Report Bugs to Apple Window*
Choose Safari > Preferences	*Access/Show Preferences Window*
Choose Safari > Block Pop-Up Windows	*Turn Block Pop Up Windows Off* or *Turn Block Pop Up Windows On*
Choose Safari > Private Browsing	*Turn Private Browsing On* or *Turn Private Browsing Off*
Choose Safari > Reset Safari	*Reset Safari*
Choose Safari > Empty Cache	*Empty Safari Cache*
Choose Safari > Hide Safari	*Hide This/The Application*
Choose Safari > Hide Others	*Hide Other Applications*
Choose Safari > Show All	*Show All Applications*
Choose Safari > Quit Safari	*Quit This/The Application*
Choose File > New Window	*Make/Create New Browser Window*
Choose File > New Tab	*Make/Create A New Tab*
Choose File > Open File	*Access/Show Open File Window*
Choose File > Open Location	*Access/Show Open Location Window*
Choose File > Close Window	*Close This/The Window*
Choose File > Close All Windows	*Close All Windows*
Choose File > Close Tab	*Close This/The Tab*
Choose File > Close Other Tabs (You must hold down the Option key to see this command.)	*Hide/Close Other Tabs*
Choose File > Save As	*Access/Show Save As Window*
Choose File > Mail Contents of This Page	*Mail Contents Of This/The Page*
Choose File > Mail Link to This Page	*Mail Link To This/The Page*

table continues on next page

TABLE 7.6 *continued*

To do this:	Say this:
Choose File > Open in Dashboard	*Access Open In Dashboard Window*
Choose File > Import Bookmarks	*Access Import Bookmarks Window*
Choose File > Export Bookmarks	*Access Export Bookmarks Window*
Choose File > Print	*Print This Document*
Choose Edit > Undo	*Undo Last Action*
Choose Edit > Redo	*Redo Last Action*
Choose Edit > Cut	*Cut This/The Selection*
Choose Edit > Copy	*Copy This/The Selection*
Choose Edit > Paste	*Paste From Clipboard*
Choose Edit > Delete	*Delete This/The Selection*
Choose Edit > Select All	*Select All*
Choose Edit > Find > Google Search	*Do Web Search*
Choose Edit > Find > Find	*Show Find Toolbar*
Choose Edit > Find > Find Next	*Find Next*
Choose Edit > Find > Find Previous	*Find Previous*
Choose Edit > Find > Hide Find Banner	*Hide/Close Find Banner*
Choose Edit > Find > Use Selection for Find	*Use Selection For Find*
Choose Edit > Find > Jump to Selection	*Jump To Selection*
Choose Edit > Spelling and Grammar > Show Spelling and Grammar	*Show Spelling And Grammar Window*
Choose Edit > Spelling and Grammar > Hide Spelling and Grammar	*Hide/Close Spelling And Grammar Window*
Choose Edit > Spelling and Grammar > Check Document Now	*Check Spelling And Grammar Of This Document*
Choose Edit > Spelling and Grammar > Check Spelling While Typing	*Turn Check Spelling While Typing Off* or *Turn Check Spelling While Typing On*
Choose Edit > Spelling and Grammar > Check Grammar With Spelling	*Turn Check Grammar With Spelling Off* or *Turn Check Grammar With Spelling On*
Choose Edit > Special Characters	*Display Special Characters Window*
Choose View > Show Toolbar	*Access/Show Toolbar*
Choose View > Hide Toolbar	*Hide/Close Toolbar*
Choose View > Customize Toolbar	*Access Customize Toolbar Window*
Choose View > Show Bookmarks Bar	*Show Bookmarks Bar*
Choose View > Hide Bookmarks Bar	*Hide/Close Bookmarks Bar*

TABLE 7.6 *continued*

To do this:	Say this:
Choose View > Show Tab Bar	*Access/Show Tab Bar*
Choose View > Hide Tab Bar	*Hide/Close Tab Bar*
Choose View > Show Status Bar	*Show Status Bar*
Choose View > Hide Status Bar	*Hide/Close Status Bar*
Choose View > Stop	*Stop Loading This/The Page*
Choose View > Reload Page	*Reload This/The Page*
Choose View > View Source	*View Source For This/The Page*
Choose History > Show All History	*Show All History*
Choose History > Back	*Jump Back*
Choose History > Forward	*Jump Forward*
Choose History > Home	*Jump Home*
Choose History > Search Results SnapBack	*Search SnapBack*
Choose History > Reopen Last Closed Window	*Reopen Last Closed Window*
Choose History > Reopen All Windows from Last Session	*Reopen All Windows From Last Session*
Choose History > Clear History	*Clear History*
Go to a specific bookmark on the bookmark bar. (For this voice command, bookmarks are numbered 1 – 9.)	*Jump To Bookmark* n
Choose Bookmarks > Show All Bookmarks	*Show All Bookmarks*
Choose Bookmarks > Hide All Bookmarks	*Hide All Bookmarks*
Choose Bookmarks > Add Bookmark	*Access Add Bookmark Window*
Choose Bookmarks > Add Bookmarks for These Tabs	*Add Bookmark For These Tabs*
Choose Bookmarks > Add Bookmark Folder	*Add Bookmark Folder*
In Bookmarks view, open the selected bookmark	*Open Selected Bookmark*
In Bookmarks view, deletes the selected bookmarks	*Delete Selected Bookmarks*
Choose Window > Minimize	*Minimize This/The Window*
Choose Window > Minimize All (You must hold down the Option key to see this command.)	*Minimize All Windows*
Choose Window > Zoom	*Zoom This/The Window*
Choose Window > Select Previous Tab	*Select Previous Tab*
Choose Window > Select Next Tab	*Select Next Tab*
Choose Window > Move Tab to New Window	*Move Tab To New Window*
Choose Window > Merge All Windows	*Merge All Windows*

table continues on next page

TABLE 7.6 *continued*

To do this:	Say this:
Choose Window > Activity	*Show Activity Window*
Choose Window > Bring All to Front	*Bring All Windows To Front*
Choose Help > Safari Help	*Display Safari Help*
Choose Help > Show Acknowledgements	*Access/Show Acknowledgements* or *Display License*
Choose Help > Installed Plug-ins	*Display Installed Plug ins*
Create a Dragon Dictate global bookmark command for the current page (page 123)	*Create A Command For This Page*
Move to the next editable text field on the page	*Move To Next Text Field*
Move to the previous editable text field on the page	*Move To Previous Text Field*
Scroll up a small amount	*Scroll Up*
Scroll down a small amount	*Scroll Down*
Scroll down a full screen	*Scroll One Screen Down*
Scroll up a full screen	*Scroll One Screen Up*
Scroll to the bottom of the page	*Scroll To Bottom*
Scroll to the top of the page	*Scroll To Top*
Scroll left a small amount	*Scroll Left*
Scroll right a small amount	*Scroll Right*
Scroll left a full screen	*Scroll One Screen Left*
Scroll right a full screen	*Scroll One Screen Right*

Mail Commands

Dragon Dictate includes support for many Mac OS X Mail commands, making it an excellent tool for dictating email messages. Table 7.7 lists the commands tested with Mail 5, the version that's part of Mac OS X Lion. You should have success with these commands in other versions of Mail as well.

TABLE 7.7 Mail Commands

To do this:	Say this:
Choose Mail > About Mail	*About This/The Application*
Choose Mail > Preferences	*Access/Show Preferences Window*
Choose Mail > Hide Mail	*Hide This/The Application*
Choose Mail > Hide Others	*Hide Other Applications*
Choose Mail > Show All	*Show All Applications*
Choose Mail > Quit Mail	*Quit This/The Application*
Choose File > New Message	*Make/Create New Message*
Choose File > New Viewer Window	*New Viewer Window*
Choose File > Close	*Close This/The Window*
Choose File > Save As	*Access/Show Save As Window*
Choose File > Attach Files	*Access/Show Attach File Window*
Choose File > Save Attachments	*Access/Show Save Attachments Window*
Choose File > Add Account	*Access/Show Add Account Window*
Choose File > Import Mailboxes	*Access/Show Import Mailboxes Window*
Choose File > Print	*Print This/The Document*
Choose Edit > Undo	*Undo Last Action*
Choose Edit > Redo	*Redo Last Action*
Choose Edit > Cut	*Cut This/The Selection*
Choose Edit > Copy	*Copy This/The Selection*
Choose Edit > Paste	*Paste From Clipboard*
Choose Edit > Delete	*Delete This/The Selection*
Choose Edit > Select All	*Select All*
Choose Edit > Complete	*Complete Entry*
Choose Edit > Paste As Quotation	*Paste As Quotation*

table continues on next page

TABLE 7.7 *continued*

To do this:	Say this:
Choose Edit > Paste And Match Style	***Paste And Match Style***
Choose Edit > Append Selected Messages	***Append Selected Messages/Email***
Choose Edit > Add Link	***Access/Show Add Hyperlink Window***
Choose Edit > Attachments > Include Original Attachments in Reply	***Include Original Attachments In Reply*** or ***Exclude Original Attachments In Reply***
Choose Edit > Find > Find	***Access Find Window***
Choose Edit > Find > Find Next	***Find Next***
Choose Edit > Find > Find Previous	***Find Previous***
Choose Edit > Find > Use Selection for Find	***Use Selection For Find***
Choose Edit > Find > Jump to Selection	***Jump To Selection***
Choose Edit > Spelling and Grammar > Show Spelling and Grammar	***Show Spelling Window***
Choose Edit > Spelling and Grammar > Check Document Now	***Check Spelling***
Choose Edit > Spelling and Grammar > Check Spelling > While Typing	***Turn Check Spelling As You Type Off*** or ***Turn Check Spelling As You Type On***
Choose Edit > Spelling and Grammar > Check Spelling > Before Sending	***Turn Check Spelling When You Click Send On***
Choose View > Sort By > Attachments	***Sort By Attachments***
Choose View > Sort By > Date	***Sort By Date Sent***
Choose View > Sort By > Flags	***Sort By Flags***
Choose View > Sort By > From	***Sort By From***
Choose View > Sort By > Size	***Sort By Size***
Choose View > Sort By > Subject	***Sort By Subject***
Choose View > Sort By > To	***Sort By To***
Choose View > Message > All Headers	***Show Long Headers***
Choose View > Message > Default Headers	***Show Default Headers***
Choose View > Message > Raw Source	***Access/Show Raw Source For Selection***
Choose View > Message > Plain Text Alternative	***Access/Show Plain Text Alternative***
Choose View > Message > Previous Alternative	***Access/Show Previous Alternative***
Choose View > Message > Next Alternative	***Access/Show Next Alternative***
Choose View > Message > Best Alternative	***Access/Show Best Alternative For Selected Message***
Choose View > Display Selected Messages Only	***Access/Show Selected Messages Only***
Choose View > Display All Messages	***Display All Messages/Email***

table continues on next page

TABLE 7.7 *continued*

To do this:	Say this:
Choose View > Hide Deleted Messages	*Hide Deleted Messages/Emails*
Choose View > Show Deleted Messages	*Access/Show Deleted Messages*
Choose View > Hide Toolbar	*Hide Toolbar*
Choose View > Show Toolbar	*Access/Show Toolbar*
Choose View > Customize Toolbar	*Access Customize Toolbar Window*
Choose Mailbox > Take All Accounts Online	*Go Online*
Choose Mailbox > Take All Accounts Offline	*Go Offline*
Choose Mailbox > Get All New Mail	*Get All New Mail*
Choose Mailbox > Synchronize All Accounts	*Synchronize All Accounts*
Choose Mailbox > Erase Deleted Items > In All Accounts	*Erase Deleted Messages/Email In All Accounts*
Choose Mailbox > Erase Deleted Items > On My Mac	*Erase Deleted Messages/Email On My Mac*
Choose Mailbox > Erase Junk Mail	*Erase Junk Mail*
Choose Mailbox > New Mailbox	*Make/Create New Mailbox*
Choose Mailbox > New Smart Mailbox	*Make/Create New Smart Mailbox*
Choose Mailbox > Edit Smart Mailbox	*Edit Selected Smart Mailbox*
Choose Mailbox > New Smart Mailbox Folder	*Make/Create New Smart Mailbox Folder*
Choose Mailbox > Rename Mailbox	*Rename Selected Mailbox*
Choose Mailbox > Delete Mailbox	*Delete This/The Mailbox*
Choose Mailbox > Go To Favorite Mailbox > Inbox	*Access/Show Inbox*
Choose Mailbox > Use This Mailbox For > Drafts	*Use This/The Mailbox For Drafts*
Choose Mailbox > Use This Mailbox For > Sent	*Use This/The Mailbox For Sent Mail/Messages*
Choose Mailbox > Use This Mailbox For > Trash	*Use This/The Mailbox For Trash*
Choose Mailbox > Use This Mailbox For > Junk	*Use This/The Mailbox For Junk*
Choose Mailbox > Rebuild	*Rebuild Selected Mailbox*
Choose Message > Send	*Send This/The Message/Email*
Choose Message > Send Again	*Send This/The Message/Email Again*
Choose Message > Reply	*Reply To This/The Message/Email*
Choose Message > Reply All	*Reply All To This/The Message/Email*
Choose Message > Reply With iChat	*Reply With I Chat*
Choose Message > Forward	*Forward Selection*
Choose Message > Forward As Attachment	*Forward This/The Message/Email*
Choose Message > Redirect	*Redirect This/The Message/Email*

table continues on next page

TABLE 7.7 *continued*

To do this:	Say this:
Choose Message > Mark > As Unread	*Mark As Unread*
Choose Message > Mark > As Read	*Mark As Read*
Choose Message > Mark > As Junk	*Mark As Junk*
Choose Message > Mark > As Low Priority	*Mark As Low Priority*
Choose Message > Mark > As Normal Priority	*Mark As Normal Priority*
Choose Message > Mark > As High Priority	*Mark As High Priority*
Choose Message > Move To "*mailbox name*" Again	*Move To Last Used Mailbox*
Choose Message > Apply Rules	*Apply Rules*
Choose Message > Add Sender to Address Book	*Add Sender To Address Book*
Choose Message > Remove Attachments	*Remove Attachments*
Choose Format > Font > Show Fonts	*Access/Show Font Palette*
Choose Format > Font > Hide Fonts	*Hide Fonts Palette*
Choose Format > Show Colors	*Show Color Palette*
Choose Format > Hide Colors	*Hide Color Palette*
Choose Format > Style > Bold	*Make Selection Bold*
Choose Format > Style > Italic	*Make Selection Italic*
Choose Format > Style > Underline	*Make Selection Underline*
Choose Format > Style > Outline	*Make/Create Selection Outline*
Choose Format > Style > Bigger	*Make Selection Bigger*
Choose Format > Style > Smaller	*Make Selection Smaller*
Choose Format > Style > Copy Style	*Copy Style of Selection*
Choose Format > Style > Paste Style	*Paste Style*
Choose Format > Style > Styles	*Access/Show Styles Window*
Choose Format > Alignment > Align Left	*Align Selection Left*
Choose Format > Alignment > Center	*Align Selection Center*
Choose Format > Alignment > Justify	*Justify Selection*
Choose Format > Alignment > Align Right	*Align Section Right*
Choose Format > Alignment > Writing Direction > Left to Right	*Change Writing Direction From Left To Right*
Choose Format > Alignment > Writing Direction > Right to Left	*Change Writing Direction From Right To Left*
Choose Format > Quote Level > Increase	*Increase Quote Level*
Choose Format > Quote Level > Decrease	*Decrease Quote Level*

table continues on next page

TABLE 7.7 *continued*

To do this:	Say this:
Choose Format > Make Plain Text	*Make Plain Text*
Choose Format > Make Rich Text	*Make Rich Text*
Choose Window > Minimize	*Minimize This/The Window*
Choose Window > Zoom	*Zoom This/The Window*
Choose Window > Message Viewer	*Access/Show Message Viewer*
Choose Window > Address Panel	*Access/Show Address Panel*
Choose Window > Previous Recipients	*Access/Show Previous Recipients*
Choose Window > Activity	*Show Activity Viewer*
Choose Window > Connection Doctor	*Access/Show Connection Doctor*
Choose Window > Bring All to Front	*Bring All Windows To Front*
Choose Help > Mail Help	*Access/Show Mail Help*
Choose Help > What's New In Mail?	*Display What's New In Mail*
Move to the beginning of a message	*Move To Beginning Of Message/Email*
Move to the end of a message	*Move To End Of Message/Email*
Move down one page	*Move Down One Page*
Move up one page	*Move Up One Page*
Move down one paragraph	*Move Down One Paragraph*
Move up one paragraph	*Move Up One Paragraph*
Move left one word	*Move Left One Word*
Move right one word	*Move Right One Word*
Move to the beginning of the line	*Move To Beginning Of This/The Line*
Move to the end of the line	*Move To End Of This Line*
Move left one character	*Move Left One Character*
Move right one character	*Move Right One Character*
Extend the selection to the beginning of the message	*Extend Selection To Beginning Of Message/Email*
Extend the selection to the end of the message	*Extend Selection To End Of Message/Email*
Extend the selection to the end of the window	*Extend Selection To End Of This/The Window*
Extend the selection down one page	*Extend Selection Down One Page*
Extend the selection up one page	*Extend Selection Up One Page*
Extend the selection to the end of the paragraph	*Extend Selection To End Of Paragraph*
Extend the selection up one paragraph	*Extend Selection Up One Paragraph*

table continues on next page

TABLE 7.7 *continued*

To do this:	Say this:
Extend the selection to the beginning of the word	*Extend Selection To Beginning Of Word*
Extend the selection to the end of the word	*Extend Selection To End Of Word*
Extend the selection up one line	*Extend Selection Up One Line*
Extend the selection down one line	*Extend Selection Down One Line*
Extend the selection to the beginning of the line	*Extend Selection To Beginning Of Line*
Extend the selection to the end of the line	*Extend Selection To End Of Line*
Extend the selection left one character	*Extend Selection Left One Character*
Extend the selection right one character	*Extend Selection Right One Character*

iCal Commands

Dragon Dictate's built-in command set includes quite a few commands for working with iCal, making it possible to use Dictate to create and work with calendars and calendar events. The commands in Table 7.8 were tested with iCal 5, the version that's part of Mac OS X Lion.

TABLE 7.8 iCal Commands

To do this:	Say this:
Choose iCal > About iCal	*About This Application*
Choose iCal > Preferences	*Access Preferences Window*
Choose iCal > Hide iCal	*Hide This Application*
Choose iCal > Hide Others	*Hide Other Applications*
Choose iCal > Show All	*Show All Applications*
Choose iCal > Quit iCal	*Quit This Application*
Choose File > New Event	*Make New Event*
Choose File > New Calendar Group	*Make New Calendar Group*
Choose File > Close	*Close This Window*
Choose File > Save As	*Access/Show Save As Window*
Choose File > Attach Files	*Access/Show Attach File Window*
Choose File > Save Attachments	*Access/Show Save Attachments Window*
Choose File > Add Account	*Access/Show Add Account Window*
Choose File > Import Mailboxes	*Access/Show Import Mailboxes Window*
Choose Edit > Undo	*Undo Last Action*
Choose Edit > Redo	*Redo Last Action*
Choose Edit > Cut	*Cut Selection*
Choose Edit > Copy	*Copy Selection*
Choose Edit > Paste	*Paste Selection*
Choose Edit > Delete	*Delete Selection*
Choose Edit > Select All	*Select All*
Choose Edit > Duplicate	*Duplicate Selection*
Choose Edit > Find	*Put Focus In Find Field*
Choose Edit > Special Characters	*Display Special Characters Palette*

table continues on next page

TABLE 7.8 *continued*

To do this:	Say this:
Choose Calendar > Subscribe	*Access Subscribe Window*
Choose Calendar > Publish	*Publish This Calendar*
Choose Calendar > Unpublish	*Unpublish This Calendar*
Choose Calendar > Send Publish Email	*Access Send Publish Email Window*
Choose Calendar > Refresh	*Refresh This Calendar*
Choose Calendar > Refresh All	*Refresh All Calendars*
Choose Calendar > Find Subscriptions	*Find Subscriptions*
Choose View > By Day	*Switch To Day View*
Choose View > By Week	*Switch To Week View*
Choose View > By Month	*Switch To Month View*
Choose View > Go To Today	*Go To Today*
Choose View > Go To Date	*Go To Date*
Choose View > Show Notifications	*Show Notifications*
Choose View > Hide Notifications	*Hide Notifications*
Choose View > Show Search Results	*Show Search Results*
Choose View > Hide Search Results	*Hide Search Results*
Choose View > Show All-Day Events	*Show All Day Events* or *Hide All Day Events*
Choose Window > Minimize	*Minimize This Window*
Choose Window > Zoom	*Zoom This Window*
Choose Window > iCal	*Show Calendar*
Choose Window > Address Panel	*Show Address Panel* or *Hide Address Panel*
Choose Window > Bring All to Front	*Bring All Windows To Front*
Choose Help > iCal Help	*Display Help*
Choose Help > Keyboard Shortcuts	*Display Keyboard Shortcuts*

Sharing on Social Networks

Dragon Dictate has several global commands (Table 7.9) that you can use to post dictated text to Twitter or Facebook. This makes it possible to update your Twitter timeline or Facebook status without going to the Twitter or Facebook website or using client software.

TIP To use Dictate's social networking sharing features, you need to connect your Twitter or Facebook account to Dictate in Dictate's sharing preferences. I explain how in the section titled "Sharing Preferences" on page 139.

TABLE 7.9 Twitter & Facebook Commands

To do this:	Say this:
Post selected text to Twitter	*Post That To Twitter* or *Post That To My Twitter Page* or *Twitter That* or *Tweet That*
Post selected text to Facebook	*Post That To Facebook* or *Post That To My Facebook Page* or *Post That To My Facebook Wall* or *Facebook That*
Dictate into a Post To Twitter dialog	*Post To Twitter* or *Post To My Twitter Page* or *Update My Twitter Page*
Dictate into a Share On Facebook dialog	*Post To Facebook* or *Update My Facebook Page* or *Update My Facebook Wall* or *Post To My Facebook Page*
Send the Twitter update in the Post To Twitter dialog	*Press Tweet*
Send the Facebook update in the Share on Facebook dialog	*Press Update*
Cancel the update	*Press Cancel*

To update a social networking site with existing dictated text:

1. In any document window, dictate the text you want to use to update Twitter or Facebook.

TIP Keep in mind that Twitter limits updates, or "tweets," to 140 characters. Anything more than that will be truncated.

2. Use one of the selection commands (Table 4.3, page 53) to select the text you want to post as an update **A**.

3. Do one of the following:

   ▸ To post the text to Twitter, say *Post That To Twitter*. When the Post To Twitter dialog appears **B**, say *Press Tweet*.

   ▸ To post the text to Facebook, say *Post That To Facebook*. When the Share on Facebook dialog appears, say *Press Share*.

   The text is posted to your account on the service you specified.

To dictate text to update to a social networking site:

1. Do one of the following:

   ▸ To update Twitter, say *Post To Twitter*.

   ▸ To update Facebook, say *Post To Facebook*.

   The appropriate update dialog appears **C**.

2. Dictate the text you want to post. It appears in the window **D**.

3. Do one of the following:

   ▸ To post to Twitter, say *Press Tweet*.

   ▸ To post to Facebook, say *Press Share*.

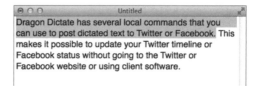

A In this example, I've dictated into a Note Pad window and selected the text I want to tweet.

B Saying Post That To Twitter puts the selected text in a dialog you can use to send it to Twitter.

C You can also display an empty Post To Twitter window, ...

D ... dictate into that, and send the tweet.

Customizing the Command Set

If the commands that are built into Dragon Dictate aren't enough for you, you can modify Dictate's command set to add your own commands.

Dictate is extremely flexible, enabling you to create simple commands that merely open a file or folder or more complex commands based on AppleScripts or Automator actions. By adding your own commands, you can control any application on your computer with your voice.

This chapter starts by telling you more about the kinds of commands Dictate supports. It explains how you can use the Commands window to manage Dictate's command set. It shows you how to add, modify, or delete commands. Finally, it explains how to export and import commands so they can be shared with other Dictate users.

In This Chapter

Command Overview

Dragon Dictate supports nine types of commands:

- **AppleScript** commands run scripts written in the AppleScript scripting language.
- **Application** commands launch specific applications.
- **Bookmark** commands open specific URLs in your default web browser.
- **File or Folder** commands open specific files or folders.
- **Menu Item** commands open specific menu items in the active application. These commands are application-specific, like the built-in application commands in Chapter 7.
- **Shell Script** commands execute a Unix shell script. This does not open the Terminal application or show any command feedback.
- **Text Macro** commands insert text you specify at the insertion point. This is a good way to quickly enter large blocks of boilerplate text.
- **Automator Workflow** commands run workflows created with the Automator application.
- **Keystroke** commands "press" specific keys or key combinations.

In each instance, you activate a command by saying its name. If the command is available—for example, if the appropriate application is active for a menu item command or if a text document is active for a text macro command—the command is invoked.

TIP Dictate fully supports AppleScript—in face, many of Dictate's built-in commands are AppleScript commands.

TIP As discussed in the section titled "Command Preferences" on page 137, you can set dictate to automatically generate commands to launch applications on your computer and enable the Web 100 Global Commands.

Managing Commands

You manage Dragon Dictate's commands in the Commands window **Ⓐ**. This window has three columns:

- The **contexts** list column lists all of the applications or contexts for which commands have been defined. If a command works in all applications, it is assigned a Global context.

- The **commands** list column lists the commands for the selected context.

- The **command settings** column displays the settings for the selected command.

Commands can be built-in or user defined. Although you cannot delete or modify a built-in command, you can duplicate it and make changes to the copy or deactivate it. This might come in handy if you want a verbal command to perform a different task.

Contexts   *Commands*   *Command settings*

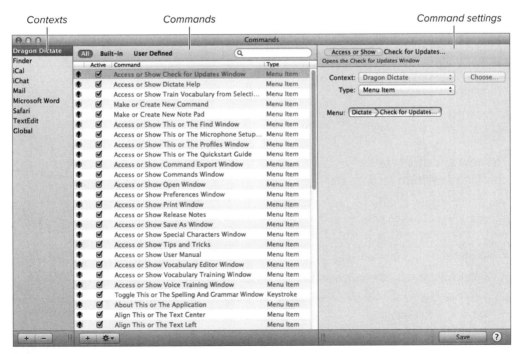

Ⓐ The Commands window with the Dragon Dictate context selected.

To open the Commands window:

Use one of the following techniques:

- Say *Access Commands Window* or *Show Commands Window*.

- Choose Tools > Commands, or press Command-K.

To close the Commands window:

1. Use one of the following techniques:

   ▶ Say *Close This Window*.

   ▶ Click the window's close button.

   ▶ Choose File > Close or press Command-W.

2. If you made changes to commands in the window, a confirmation dialog appears . Click Save to save your changes.

   The window closes.

To display the commands for a specific context:

In the context list column of the Commands window Ⓐ, click the name of the context you want to view commands for.

The commands for that context appear in the commands column Ⓐ.

To show specific types of commands within a context:

In the Commands window Ⓐ, click the button at the top of the commands column for the type of commands you want to display:

- **All** displays all commands Ⓐ.

- **Built-In** displays built-in commands.

- **User Defined** displays the commands you added to Dictate.

Ⓑ If you made changes in the window, Dictate asks if you want to save them.

C In this example, I'm searching for Mail commands related to attachments.

D In this example, I've selected one of the Dragon Dictate commands.

E The tools menu offers options to delete or duplicate a selected command.

F The duplicate command appears beneath the original.

To search for a specific command:

1. In the context column of the Commands window, select the application or context where you expect to find the command.

2. In the commands column, click a button to display the type of command you expect it to be. If you're not sure whether it's a built-in or user-defined command, click All.

3. Enter a search word or phrase in the search box at the top of the window **C**.

   Search results appear immediately in the command column **C**.

To duplicate a command:

1. Locate and select the command you want to duplicate **D**.

2. Choose Duplicate Command from the tools menu at the bottom of the window **E**.

   The command is copied and appears in the command list beneath the original command **F**.

3. Follow the instructions in the section titled "To modify command settings" on page 125 to change the settings of the duplicate command so it works the way you want it to.

TIP Duplicating a command is a great way to create a new command that does almost the same thing as an existing command. You can then modify the new command so it works the way you want it to.

To change the status of a command:

1. Locate the command you want to change the status of **C**.

2. Click the check box in the active column:

   ▸ Removing the check mark **G** deactivates the command so it can no longer be used in Dictate.

   ▸ Adding a check mark **C** activates the command so it can be used in Dictate.

TIP If you want to replace a built-in command with a custom command, you can disable the built-in command and give the custom command the same name.

To delete a command:

1. Locate and select the command you want to delete.

2. Choose Delete Command from the tools menu at the bottom of the window **E** or press the Delete key.

3. In the confirmation dialog that appears **H**, click Delete.

TIP You can't delete a built-in command. The Delete Command item on the tools menu **E** will be gray and if you press the Delete key, a dialog will tell you that the command can't be deleted **I**.

TIP If you don't want a built-in command to function, disable it as discussed in the section titled "To change the status of a command."

G Toggling a check box off disables a command.

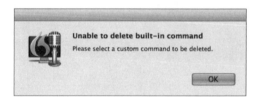

H Click Delete in this dialog to delete the command.

I If you try to delete a built-in command, Dictate scolds you.

Adding Custom Commands

You can add your own commands to Dictate so it can perform additional tasks either with applications it already supports or with other applications.

There are two ways to add a command:

- **Duplicate an existing command** (as discussed in the section titled "To duplicate a command" on page 121) and modify its options to meet your needs.

- **Create a brand new command** and set its options to meet your needs.

Before you create a command, take some time to think it out. There are three aspects to consider:

- What is the context of the command? Will it work in all applications as a Global command or just within one application?

- What will you say to trigger the command? The command name needs to be unique to the context.

- What will the command actually do? This is where the type of command (page 118) becomes very important.

If you want to create an application-specific command for an application that isn't in the Commands window's context list, you need to add that application as a context. This makes it possible for Dictate to access information about the application, if necessary, when you create a command for it. You can add a context before you add a command or add a context on the fly when you create the command.

This part of the chapter explains how to add a context, create a command, and modify command settings.

To add a context:

1. Open the Commands window.

2. Click the + button at the bottom of the context list column to display a menu .

3. Choose an option:
   - **New Application Context** displays an Open dialog **B**. Select the application you want to assign to the context and click Open.
   - **New Website Context** displays a dialog **C**. Enter a name and URL for the website associated with the context. Click Add.

   The context is added to the context list column of the Commands window **D**.

TIP The website context feature makes it possible to create commands that work only in websites with a specific base URL.

To add a new command:

Use one of the following techniques:

- Say *Make New Command* or *Create New Command*.

- Choose File > New Command, or press Shift-Command-N.

- In the Commands window, click the + button at the bottom of the commands list column.

If the Commands list window wasn't already open, it opens. A new command named *Command Name* appears in the commands list **E**.

TIP If a context was selected when you added the command, the command is automatically assigned to that context **E**. You can change this setting if you need to.

A Choose the command for the type of context you want.

B Use this Open dialog to select the application you want to create a context for.

C To create a website context, enter the name and URL for the website's main page.

D In this example, I created a website context for my blog (An Eclectic Mind) and an application context for Evernote.

E Here's a new command I created for Evernote.

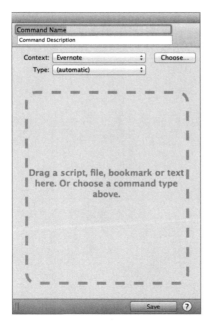

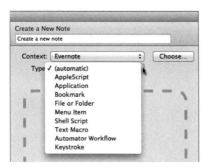

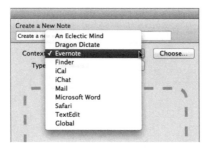 Set options for a command here.

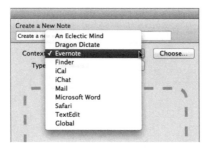 Choose a context from this menu.

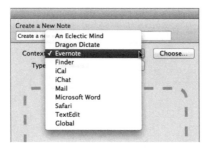 Choose a command type from the Type menu.

To modify command settings:

1. In the Commands window, select the command you want to modify settings for **E**.

2. In the command settings column on the right side of the window **F**, set basic options:

   ▸ **Command Name** is the words you'll speak to trigger the command. This must be unique for every command in that context and can't be the same as a global command.

   ▸ **Command Description** is a description of what the command does. This can help you remember a command's function. This field is also used when you search for a command (page 121).

   ▸ **Context** is the command's context. Choose an option from the pop-up menu **G**. The menu will include all existing contexts. If the context you need is not in the list, you can click the Choose button and use the Open dialog that appears **B** to select one. This creates a new context on the fly.

   ▸ **Type** is the type of command (page 118). Choose an option from the pop-up menu **H**. Your choice will have a direct impact on the remaining options in the dialog.

   TIP If you're going to create an AppleScript, Application, Bookmark, File or Folder, Shell Script, Text Macro, or Automator Workflow command leave the type set to *(automatic)*.

   continues on next page

3. Do one of the following:

▸ To create an AppleScript, Shell Script, Text Macro, or Automator Workflow, command, drag the icon for the script, text file, or from the Finder window into the Commands window beneath the Type menu 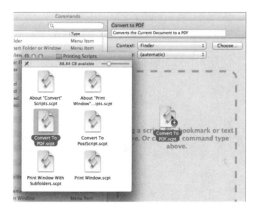. The file's content or path is copied into the window and the Type is set accordingly **J**.

▸ To create a Bookmark command, drag the URL from the address bar of your web browser window into the Commands window beneath the Type menu **K**. The URL is copied to a field there and the Type is set accordingly **L**.

▸ To create an Application or File or Folder command, drag the item's icon from the Finder window into the Commands window beneath the Type menu. The name of the application or the path to the file or folder is copied to a field there and the Type is set accordingly **M**.

I Drag the icon for an AppleScript...

J ... to enter that script into the Commands window.

K You can also drag a URL from a web browser's address bar...

L ... to enter that URL into the Commands window.

M Dragging a folder to the area beneath the Type menu adds the path to that folder.

N Select the menu item you want to assign to the Menu command.

O The menu item is added to the Commands window.

- ▸ To create a Menu command, click the Select a menu item button beneath the Type menu to display a menu of available commands **N** and choose the command you want. The menu item you chose appears beneath the Type menu **O**.

TIP If the application the context is for is not already running, click the Launch Context button in the Commands window **N** to open the application before clicking the Select a menu item button.

- ▸ To create a Keystroke command, click the + beneath the Keystroke list and set options in the area beside it. You can repeat this process to create a Keystroke command that consists of multiple keystrokes **P**; drag a keystroke up or down in the list to change the order in which they are pressed.

4. Click Save to save your settings.

P In this example, I've effectively created a macro that moves the selected item to the Trash and empties the Trash—all with a single voice command.

Importing & Exporting Commands

Commands are stored in a user's profile file. If you have multiple profile files—perhaps you have Dragon Dictate installations on multiple computers—or if you want to share your commands with other Dictate users, you can export commands from one file and import them into another. You do this with the Command Export and Command Import commands. Here's how.

To export commands:

1. Choose File > Command Export .

   The Command Export window appears. It lists all of the contexts for which there are commands. Clicking a disclosure triangle beside a context name displays the context's commands **B**.

2. Toggle check boxes to select the commands you want to export.

3. Click the Export button.

4. Use the Save Exported Command Set dialog **C** to name and choose a disk location for the exported commands.

5. Click Save.

   The commands are saved in a specially formatted text file.

6. Click OK in the Command Export dialog that appears **D** to dismiss it.

A The File menu includes three commands for importing or exporting Dictate commands.

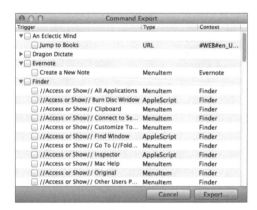

B The Command Export window lists all of the commands you can export.

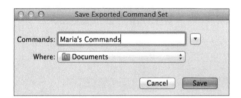

C Enter a name and specify a disk location for the exported commands file.

D Dictate tells you when the commands have been successfully exported.

E Use the Import a Command Set dialog to locate and select the command file you want to import.

F Dictate tells you when the import process has been successfully completed.

To import commands:

1. Choose File > Command Import **A**.

2. Use the Import a Command Set dialog that appears **E** to locate and select the commands file you want to import.

3. Click Select Command Set.

4. If a second dialog appears, prompting you to Import Trigger Terms for a Command Set, click Cancel.

5. Wait while the commands are imported into the profile file.

6. Click OK in the Command Import dialog that appears **F**.

TIP The ScriptPak Import command, which can also be found on the File menu **A**, enables you to import commands that were exported from another dictation program called iListen. This command works very much like the Command Import feature.

Setting Preferences

Like most other Mac OS applications, Dragon Dictate offers a number of preference settings that enable users to customize the way it works. These settings are broken down in to seven categories:

- General
- Appearance
- Dictation
- Recognition
- Command
- Shortcuts
- Sharing

This chapter explains what each preference setting does and how it changes the way Dictate works. It also tells you how you can set Dictate options so it works best for you.

In This Chapter

The Preferences Window

All of Dragon Dictate's preferences can be found in its Preferences window. Simply open the window and click the button for the category of preferences you want to view or change. Any changes you make to preferences are automatically saved when you close the window.

TIP You can click the Help button (a question mark icon) at the bottom of any preferences pane to learn more about its options.

To open the Preferences window:

With Dictate active, use one of the following techniques:

- Say *Access Preferences Window* or *Show Preferences Window*.

- Choose Dictate > Preferences 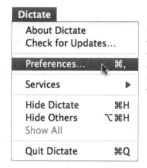, or press Command-, (comma).

The Preferences window appears. It displays the last preferences pane you viewed.

To close the Preferences window:

With the Preferences window active, use one of the following techniques:

- Say *Close This Window*.

- Click the window's close button.

- Choose File > Close, or press Command-W.

A You can open the Preferences window by choosing Preferences from the Dictate menu.

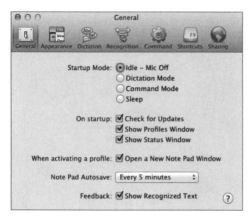

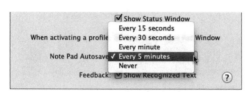

(A) The General preferences pane of Dictate's Preferences window.

(B) You can specify how long Dictate should wait before automatically saving the currently open Note Pad file.

(C) Dictate can display the dictation it recognizes beneath the Status window.

General Preferences

Dragon Dictate's General preferences (A) control a number of general usage options:

- **Startup Mode** enables you to specify what mode Dictate should be in when you start it. If you select Idle - Mic Off, you'll need to turn the microphone on with a click, menu command, or shortcut key before using Dictate.

- **On startup** lets you specify what actions Dictate should perform. You can toggle any combination of check boxes:

  ▸ **Check for Updates** goes online to check for software updates.

  ▸ **Show Profiles Window** displays the Profiles window so you can choose the profile you want to use.

  ▸ **Show Status Window** displays the Status window.

- **When activating a profile Open a New Note Pad Window** automatically opens a Note Pad window when you open a profile.

- **Note Pad Autosave** (B) enables you to specify the amount of time Dictate waits before automatically saving the Note Pad document. If you choose Never from the pop-up menu, the Autosave feature is disabled.

- **Feedback Show Recognized Text** displays dictated text and commands that Dictate recognizes under the Status window (C). This can help you understand why Dictate reacted unexpectedly if it does.

Appearance Preferences

Appearance preferences 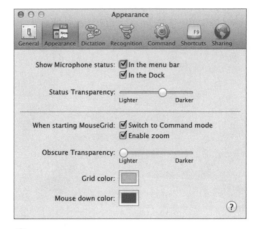, as you might have guessed, control certain aspects of the appearance of Dragon Dictate's interface.

- **Show Microphone Status** lets you specify where to display status icons:
  - ▶ **In the menu bar** displays the status among icons on the menu bar **B**.
  - ▶ **In the Dock** displays the status in Dictate's Dock icon **C**.
- **Status Transparency** controls the transparency of the Status window. Lighter is more transparent than Darker.
- **When starting MouseGrid** offers two options for what should happen when you use the mouse grid feature:
  - ▶ **Switch to Command mode** switches Dictate to Command mode—which makes sense since that's the mode you use with the mouse grid.
  - ▶ **Enable zoom** enables the zoom feature when the mouse grid is activating a small part of the screen **D**.
- **Obscure Transparency** sets the transparency of the rest of the window when you're using the mouse grid feature. Lighter is more transparent than darker.
- **Grid color** is the color of the mouse grid. Click the color well to display a standard Colors palette **E** and choose the color you want.
- **Mouse down color** is the color of the pulsating circle that appears when you use the *Mouse Hold* command. Click the color well to display the Colors palette **E** and choose the color you want.

A The Appearance preferences pane.

B C You can display the microphone status in the menu bar (top) or Dock (bottom). Both of these examples show that my microphone is sleeping.

D This example shows the mouse grid feature with zoom enabled.

E Use a standard Colors palette to choose a color.

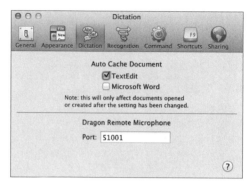

A The Dictation Preferences pane.

Dictation Preferences

Dictation preferences **A** control some aspects of how Dragon Dictate works with specific applications and the remote microphone app for iPad and iPhone.

- **Auto Cache Document** is a feature that makes it possible to mix dictation with manual editing in certain applications. This is naturally supported in Dictate's Note Pad, but can also be enabled in TextEdit and Microsoft Word by toggling one or both of these check boxes on.

  TIP If you haven't yet done so, read the section titled "The Golden Rule" on page 48. It has very important information about mixing dictation with manual editing in documents.

- **Dragon Remote Microphone Port** is a setting for use with the Dragon Remote Microphone app. (Because this app is not part of the Dictate application, it's covered briefly in Appendix B.)

Recognition Preferences

Recognition preferences 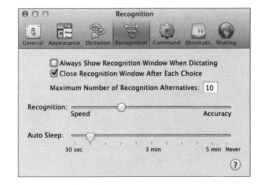 help you fine-tune how Dragon Dictate recognizes what you say and how its Recognition window **B** works.

- **Always Show Recognition Window When Dictating** displays the recognition window whenever you dictate.

- **Close Recognition Window After Each Choice** automatically hides the window after you choose one of its options.

- **Maximum Number of Recognition Alternatives** lets you set a value for the most options that should appear in the Recognition window.

- **Recognition** lets you set a slider to trade off between speed and accuracy of voice recognition. If you naturally speak slowly and have many pauses, you might want to set this closer to Accuracy. But if you speak quickly and need Dictate to keep up with you, you might prefer it set closer to Speed. Experiment with this feature to get the best setting for the way you dictate.

- **Auto Sleep** lets you determine how long Dictate will wait for dictation before it automatically puts the microphone to sleep. Set this for the way you use Dictate. Remember, you can always simply say *Wake Up* to resume dictation after Dictate has automatically gone to sleep.

A The Recognition preferences pane.

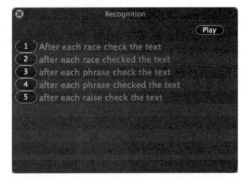

B The Recognition window can help you improve Dictate's ability to understand your voice.

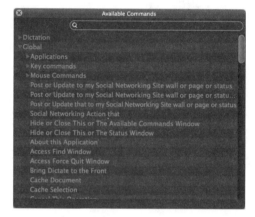

A The Command preferences pane.

B The Available Commands window lists all the commands currently available in Dictate.

Command Preferences

Dragon Dictate's Command preferences pane **A** offers options for displaying commands in the Available Commands window **B** as well as automatically generating commands on startup.

- **Available Commands Window** offers two options for that window:

  - **Show Global above Application Commands** places all global commands above application-specific commands in the window.

  - **Enable Web Site Commands** enables what Dictate calls the Web 100 Commands—a set of global commands for accessing popular Web sites. Once enabled, these commands are listed under Web 100 in the Available Commands window for reference.

- **Command Generation** instructs Dictate to automatically generate global commands for one or two functions:

  - **Generate Application Launch Commands** reads all the applications installed on your Mac and creates an **Activate** command for each one. So, for example, if you have Microsoft Excel installed on your Mac, Dictate would create the **Activate Microsoft Excel** command to launch that application.

  - **Generate Email Commands** creates global commands for creating and addressing email messages.

Shortcuts Preferences

Shortcuts preferences **A** enables you to set shortcut keys to activate a number of Dragon Dictate features:

- **Toggle Microphone** toggles the microphone on or off.

- **Select Speech Mode** cycles through each of Dictate's modes: Dictation, Command, Spelling, and Numbers.

- **Show Recognition Window** toggles the display of the Recognition window.

- **Dismiss MouseGrid** hides the mouse grid.

To set a shortcut key:

1. In the Shortcuts preferences pane **A**, click the keystroke to the right of the feature you want to set the keystroke for.

   The field becomes selected with the words *Type shortcut* in it **B**.

2. Press the key combination for the new shortcut.

   The new keystroke appears beside the feature name **C**.

A Use the Shortcut preferences pane to change shortcut keys for accessing certain features.

B In this example, I clicked the key beside Toggle Microphone.

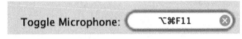

C Typing a new shortcut sets it.

A Use the Sharing preferences pane to set up Facebook and Twitter for dictated updates.

B Enter your Twitter login information in this dialog and click OK.

C A Reset button appears in the Sharing preferences pane beside a service that has been configured for use with Dictate.

Sharing Preferences

Dragon Dictate's Sharing preferences pane **A** enables you to connect with Facebook or Twitter (or both). Once enabled, you can update your Facebook status or send a Twitter tweet using verbal commands (refer to "Sharing on Social Networks" on page 115).

TIP As this book went to press, the ability to link to Facebook had "broken" with a recent Facebook update. Nuance Communication is aware of the problem and is working hard to fix it. The instructions here work with Twitter; the process will likely be similar for Facebook.

To configure a Twitter account:

1. In Sharing preferences **A**, click the Login button for Twitter.

2. A dialog appears, prompting you for your Twitter username and password **B**. Enter this information and click OK.

   Dictate goes online and logs you into Twitter. The Sharing preferences pane changes to indicate that you are now connected **C**.

TIP You can remove a Twitter connection by clicking the Reset button in the Sharing preferences pane **C**.

Menus & Shortcut Keys

This Appendix illustrates all of Dragon Dictate's menus and provides a list of corresponding shortcut keys.

To use a shortcut key, hold down the modifier key (usually Command) while pressing the keyboard key for the command.

In This Chapter

Dictate Menu

Preferences	Command-, (comma)
Hide Dictate	Command-H
Show Others	Option-Command-H
Quit Dictate	Command-Q
Quit and Discard Windows	Option-Command-Q

Dictate

About Dictate
Check for Updates...

Preferences...   ⌘,

Services   ▶

Hide Dictate   ⌘H
Hide Others   ⌥⌘H
Show All

Quit Dictate   ⌘Q

File Menu

New Note Pad	Command-N
New Command	Shift-Command-N
Open	Command-O
Close	Command-W
Close All	Option-Command-W
Save	Command-S
Save As	Shift-Command-S
Print	Command-P

File

New Note Pad   ⌘N
New Command   ⇧⌘N
Open...   ⌘O
Open Recent   ▶

Close   ⌘W
Save   ⌘S
Save As...   ⇧⌘S
Revert to Saved

Print...   ⌘P

Save Profile

Command Import...
Command Export...

ScriptPak Import...

Edit Menu

```
Edit
  Undo Typing                  ⌘Z
  Redo                        ⇧⌘Z

  Cut                          ⌘X
  Copy                         ⌘C
  Paste                        ⌘V
  Paste and Match Style    ⌥⇧⌘V
  Delete
  Select All                   ⌘A

  Find                          ▶
  Spelling                      ▶

  Special Characters...      ⌥⌘T
```

Undo	Command-Z
Redo	Shift-Command-Z
Cut	Command-X
Copy	Command-C
Paste	Command-V
Paste and Match Style	Option-Shift-Command-V
Select All	Command-A
Find	Command-F
Find Next	Command-G
Find Previous	Shift-Command-G
Use Selection for Find	Command-E
Jump to Selection	Command-J
Show Spelling and Grammar	Command-: (colon)
Check Spelling	Command-; (semicolon)
Special Characters	Option-Command-T

Speech Menu

```
Speech
  Microphone On   ⌘F11

  Dictation
✓ Command
  Spelling
  Numbers
  Sleep
```

Microphone On/ Microphone Off	Command-F11

Tools Menu

```
Tools
  Profiles...
  Commands...                  ⌘K
  Vocabulary Editor...        ⇧⌘V

  Auto Formatting...
  Microphone Setup...
  Voice Training...
  Vocabulary Training...
  Train Vocabulary from Selection...
```

Commands	Command-K
Vocabulary Editor	Shift-Command-V

Format Menu

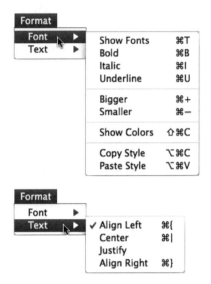

Show Fonts	Command-T
Bold	Command-B
Italic	Command-I
Underline	Command-U
Bigger	Command-+ (plus)
Smaller	Command- – (minus)
Show Colors	Shift-Command-C
Copy Style	Option-Command-C
Paste Style	Option-Command-V
Align Left	Command-{ (left brace)
Center	Command-I (bar)
Align Right	Command-} (right brace)

Window Menu

Minimize	Command-M
Minimize All	Option-Command-M
Enter Full Screen/ Exit Full Screen	Control-Command-F

Help Menu

(no shortcut keys)

Setting Up Dragon Remote Microphone

If you have an iPhone or an iPad, you can use it as a remote, wireless microphone with Dragon Dictate. Just install the free Dragon Remote Microphone app, make sure your mobile device is on the same Wi-Fi network as your computer running Dragon Dictate, and use Dictate and the app to configure your device as a microphone. You can then do all your dictation into your iPhone or iPad from anywhere within range of your network.

This appendix explains how to install Dragon Remote Microphone on an iPhone and how to configure it to work as an audio device with Dragon Dictate. These instructions should work pretty much the same way on an iPad.

Installing Dragon Remote Microphone

There are two main ways to install Dragon Remote Microphone on an iPhone:

- Use the App Store app on your iPhone to find Dragon Remote Microphone and install it directly to your phone.

- Use iTunes to find Dragon Remote Microphone app on the iTunes app store, download it to your computer, and then sync your iPhone to your computer.

These instructions cover the first method.

To install Dragon Remote Microphone on an iPhone:

1. On the iPhone, tap the App Store icon.

2. In the bottom row of buttons, tap search.

3. Enter *Dragon Microphone* in the search box at the top of the screen  and tap the Search button.

4. Dragon Remote Microphone should appear among the search results . Tap it.

5. In the description screen , tap FREE and then tap INSTALL.

6. Enter your Apple ID password if prompted and tap OK.

7. Wait while the app is downloaded and installed.

   When it's finished, an icon named Microphone appears on one of your app screens .

A Search the App Store for Dragon Microphone.

B Dragon Remote Microphone should appear among the search results.

C You can learn more on the app's description screen.

D Its icon appears on one of your phone's screens.

Ⓐ The main screen of the Dragon Remote Microphone application.

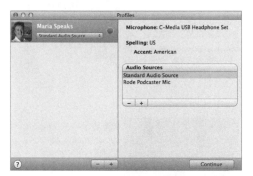

Ⓑ Start by adding an audio source to your profile.

Ⓒ Be sure to choose Dragon Remote Microphone from the pop-up menu.

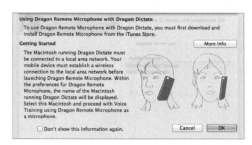

Ⓓ This window offers tips for using your iPhone with Dragon Dictate.

Configuring the Microphone App

You configure the Microphone app by setting up an audio device in Dragon Dictate on your computer and then telling the iPhone app to connect. You then complete voice training like you would for any other audio device.

To add Dragon Remote Microphone as a device to your profile file:

1. Make sure your phone is turned on and connected to the same Wi-Fi network as your computer.

2. Tap the Microphone icon on your iPhone to launch the app.

3. If a general information screen appears, tap it to display the main screen Ⓐ.

4. In the Dragon Dictate application on your Mac, choose Tools > Profiles to display the Profiles window Ⓑ.

5. Select the profile you want to add Dragon Remote Microphone to.

6. Click the + button beneath the Audio Sources list.

7. Set options in the dialog that appears Ⓒ:

   ▸ **Name** is the name of the device. You might want to name it iPhone or iPad.

   ▸ **Microphone** is the microphone you are adding. Choose Dragon Remote Microphone.

8. Click Continue.

9. A screen with information appears Ⓓ. Read it but don't click OK yet.

10. On your iPhone tap the red microphone button on the screen Ⓐ.

continues on next page

11. A window with options appears **E**. Tap Detect available computers.

12. A list of computers should appear with your profile name and computer name among them **F**. Tap your profile name.

13. Your profile name appears in the main screen **G**. Tap the red button.

14. On your Mac, a dialog asks if you want to allow a connection from your iPhone **H**. Click Allow.

15. If the information screen is still displayed on your computer **D**, click OK.

16. A Voice Training window appears. Follow the instructions in the section titled "To train Dictate to understand your voice" on page 8.

17. After initial calibration, click the red microphone button on your phone again to continue with the voice training.

18. When training is complete, Dictate tells you. Click Done in the Voice Training window.

Your iPhone is added as an audio source to your Profile **I**. You can now use it like any other audio source; just be sure to open the app and click the red microphone button **G** when you're ready to dictate.

E The app offers several options for connecting to Dragon Dictate.

F Your profile and computer name should appear in a list.

G When you tap your profile name, it appears on the main app screen.

H Click Allow to allow communication between your Mac and your iPhone.

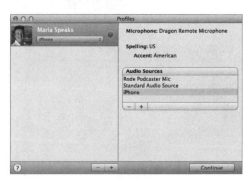

I Your iPhone is added as an audio device.

Index

L

Left Arrow command, 52

ligatures, 34, 35

Lion, 2, 17, 81, 103, 107, 113. *See also* Mac OS X

lowercase, 38, 54, 71

Lowercase commands, 38, 54

M

Mac OS commands, 80, 81

Mac OS X

   Finder commands, 96–98

   Mail commands, 107–112

   Speech preferences, 57, 58

   System Voice menu, 58

   Text to Speech feature, 57

   Universal Access features, 2

   versions, 2

macros. *See* Text Macro commands

Mail application, 26, 84

Mail commands, 107–112

mathematical symbols, 38

measurement units, 44

menu item commands, 118, 127

menus, 141–144

Microphone app, Dragon remote, 2, 135, 145–148

Microphone button, 21

Microphone menu, 5

Microphone Off command, 22

microphones. *See also* audio sources

   adjusting, 6–7

   choosing, 5

   compatibility information, 2

   connecting, 3

   sound quality considerations, 2

   turning on/off, 20, 21–22

   using multiple, 4, 5

Microphone Setup dialog, 7

Microsoft Word, 26, 49, 50, 135

Miscellaneous area, Auto Formatting dialog, 45

misspellings, 59

Mode menu, 22

modes, 20, 22, 25. *See also* specific modes

modification commands, 54

mouse clicks, 87, 90

mouse commands, 77, 87–90, 96

mouse grid, 87, 88, 134, 138

Mouse Hold command, 134

mouse pointer, 87, 89

Move commands, 52

N

Natural capitalization, 71

navigation commands, 52, 53

No Caps commands, 29

noise, 2, 7

non-Latin characters, 34, 35

non-word characters, 28

No Space commands, 30

Note Pad, 26–27, 49, 67, 133, 135

Nuance Communications, ix, 48, 73

numbers

   dictating, 20, 37–38, 39–41

   setting formatting options for, 42–46

Numbers area, Auto Formatting dialog, 44

Numbers mode, 20, 22, 25, 37

Numbers Mode command, 22

Numeral command, 38

O

ODT files, 66

P

Pages, Apple, 26
parentheses, 55
pauses, 45, 136
pausing program, 20
phone numbers, 39, 40, 43
phrases, 51, 60
Pick command, 62, 64
plain text files, 27, 66
Play the Selection command, 64
pointer, mouse, 87, 89
postal codes, 39, 41, 42
preference settings, 131–139
    appearance, 134
    command, 137
    dictation, 135
    general, 133
    recognition, 136
    sharing, 139
    shortcuts, 138
Preferences window, 132
prices, 44. *See also* currency symbols
profiles
    adding audio sources to, 12
    adding vocabulary lists to, 74
    and Auto Formatting settings, 46
    creating, 4–5
    deleting, 11
    managing, 11–13
    naming, 5
    purpose of, 4
    selecting, 13
    using multiple, 4, 5

Profiles window, 5, 6, 11
program interface, 15–23
    common tasks, 21–23
    elements, 16–19
    modes, 20, 22, 25 (*See also* specific modes)
pronunciation, 71, 72
Proofread Document command, 57
proofreading commands, 57
proper nouns, 33, 59, 65
punctuation, 28, 30, 31, 37, 55–56
punctuation commands, 31
Purge Cache command, 50
purple moon icon, 23

Q

question mark icon, 132
quotes, 55

R

Radio Alphabet, International, 34
Read Document command, 57
Read Selection command, 57, 58
Read The Document command, 57
Read The Words command, 57
Recognition preferences, 136
Recognition window, 60–64
    correcting dictated text in, 62–64
    how it works, 60
    opening/closing, 61
    playing back recording in, 64
    purpose of, 18, 60
    setting preferences for, 136
    ways of training Dictate with, 60
Redo Dictation command, 51